UNDERSTANDING ANXIETY IN EVERYDAY LIFE

Understanding Anxiety in Everyday Life

by

ERIC J. TRIMMER

London
GEORGE ALLEN AND UNWIN LTD

FIRST PUBLISHED IN 1970

ISBN 0 04 616007 8

PRINTED IN GREAT BRITAIN
in 11 on 13 pt Times type
BY CLARKE DOBLE AND BRENDON LTD
PLYMOUTH

ACKNOWLEDGEMENTS

Experts are sometimes quick to protest against any trespass on their own rather strictly confined area of activity. Those who have helped me to write this book, however, tend to agree that anxiety is a condition that can be tackled with advantage, by the generalist as well as the specialist. Well over ninety per cent of all illnesses of a psychiatric nature are first seen and dealt with in general practice. The commonest of these illnesses is anxiety. No apology is made, therefore, for a book about anxiety written by a GP, and based on observation, not dogma.

I have obtained help from many sources, some of which are itemized in the text. Particularly useful has been Professor C. H. Hardin Branch's *Aspects of Anxiety*, (J. B. Lippincott Co., Philadelphia). I have also been influenced by the philosophical ideas of Jean Gebser. A widespread scanning of modern psychiatric literature has been made possible by the Medlar's[1] Organization of the Royal Society of Medicine, without whose help the task would have been prodigious.

Various illustrative cases have been quoted throughout. These have been altered, always in unimportant detail, so that any identification is impossible.

Eric Trimmer

[1] Medical Literature Analysis and Retrieval System.

CONTENTS

Introduction

It is not always necessary to find the cause for a disease to be able to treat it effectively. For instance, the symptoms of a depressive illness can be controlled quite effectively with electro-convulsive therapy, but nobody knows why this treatment succeeds. Altering the course of a disease, however, becomes much simpler if we understand its cause.

As yet the *ultimate* cause of anxiety eludes us. Many authorities have concentrated upon certain aspects of anxiety and have made interesting and instructive detailed deductions as to its aetiology. Some, like Charles Rycroff, an analyst of more than usual lucidity, argue that anxiety is a disturbed signal of awareness that occurs because of a personality inadequacy or immaturity, buried in the unconscious mind.

Others see anxiety as fundamentally a question of altered biochemistry, perhaps a sort of 'misread' information fed into our human programming in the same way as a radio may inexplicably pick up a random morse signal from an unknown source and spoil our favourite programme.

As people have become, on the whole, better informed on scientific matters, some of the older explanations of the psychological disharmony that is anxiety become rather unconvincing in our twentieth-century materialistic and permissive society. There *are* a few people in our present-day environment who are tormented by guilt, about sex for instance, but the average man and woman can usually live his and her life to the full without being disturbed unduly on these scores and I feel these are not major causes of contemporary anxiety.

The toll taken as far as anxiety is concerned remains high. Practitioners in all types of medical work find themselves increasingly involved with the treatment of simple anxiety states and their *sequelae*. Drugs, although prescribed in immense quantities, are often disappointing when it comes to controlling anxiety, except on a short-term basis. Psychoanalysis is sometimes effective but can only help a very few people, due to the amount of time necessary for a therapeutic analysis, and the severe shortage of analysts. A compromise is *group* analysis in which several people talk over their problems jointly, with a trained psychiatrist. Simple straightforward discussion of anxiety symptoms leading to an understanding of some of the basic problems involved in its generation does seem to provide help for many sufferers, and this is really why this book was written.

Some years ago I was approached by a pharmaceutical company to write a series of articles to be used as mailing material to doctors on the subject of the aetiology, or basic cause, of anxiety. To my surprise the standard works on psychology and psychiatry offered little help in this task.

This book is an expansion of my investigations in this field in the light of subsequent experience. It is hoped that some of the ideas expressed here will help those troubled, or even disabled by anxiety to find a new freedom.

PART I

CHAPTER ONE

What is Anxiety?

If you were to ask half a dozen different people this question they would probably come back with six different answers. A man approaching the peak period in his career might say it is the feeling he gets from time to time when he wonders whether or not he will realize his ambitions. For instance: will perhaps another, younger man be promoted over his head?

A housewife, aged around fifty, might conceivably appreciate anxiety in a totally different way. The characteristic flavour of her anxiety would be strongly seasoned by the menopause. At this time, changes in hormone levels in the blood can cause many physical symptoms in women. The whole of the circulatory system becomes touchy, rather as it did during early adolescence, and she tends to suffer from sudden skin flushing as the minute vessels in the skin of the face and elsewhere suddenly dilate, like a prolonged blush. The heart is liable to inexplicable bouts of rapid action, and so palpitation is common as well. Emotions are easily disturbed in the menopause and life may be experienced in a distorted way. Joy becomes elation and simple domestic disappointments are often felt as tragedies. Anxiety at this time is usually crystallized around a physical symptom. Sometimes it centres upon some specific organ, and fears about the heart maybe or the mind are commonplace.

A younger person perhaps in the early-thirties, tends to experience anxiety in yet another way. He is more concerned with worries which relate to more tangible things. Will he be able to earn enough money to furnish his home, keep his place in society, run his car and look after his children? What would happen to his young family if he died? The woman in mid-thirties is subconsciously anxious about her children too, but also she is concerned about her husband's and her own welfare. Usually, the family has as yet made no move away from her and so she feels acutely responsible for them. Her anxiety therefore tends to be focused on what will happen to her family if they are deprived of her, their mother. When anxiety is overwhelming horrors plague her. If for instance a child is home late from school she wonders, has there been an accident? Everyday domestic events like someone coming in with wet feet, a temperature a degree or so above normal, or a cough during the night, spell disaster to her under the powerful persuasion of anxiety.

The worries of the late teens and the early-twenties are in many ways centred upon the problems of stepping into the unknown. This is really the unknown world of adult behaviour, discretion and sophistication. In both sexes at this age anxiety often manifests itself mainly by the individual turning away from these pressures, and compensating for anxious fears with aggression directed against the establishment.

At the two extremes of the age scale, the elderly and the very young, anxiety seems to be experienced in another rather special way. In older people it results in the rejection of an 'unkind' world and a retreat into isolation. In youngsters it results in a flight from responsibilities that can normally be accepted by someone within the age group in question. In other words, some previous act of growing up is jettisoned, for example bladder or bowel control, as part of an unconscious wish for return to babyhood.

Anxiety is both common and complex. In many ways it is a quite unremarkable fact of normal living.

Anxiety does have a certain part to play in, for instance, the education of young children. Quite properly a mother transmits some of her own anxiety, by the mysterious process known as empathy, to her child – so that the dangers of fire, heights, and water are appreciated. Anxiety about failure, either in one's own eyes or in the eyes of others, often stimulates the body and the psyche to greater efforts. Delegates to a symposium held at the Royal Society of Medicine recently on the subject of 'The Meaning of Physical Fitness' heard Dr Roger Bannister describe how many record-breaking athletes experience acute anxiety, even to the extent of actually vomiting before epoch-making athletic achievements. The author, a fair to middling athlete as a schoolboy, remembers such pre-performance 'nerves' extremely clearly.

Of course these 'built-in' anxiety factors that help the individual in his struggle through life are not limited to the football field or the athletics track. The biographies of actors and prominent statesmen often disclose, if they are frankly written, similar states of body and mind before important performances.

From the strictly biological point of view anxiety is usually regarded as a self-protective survival phenomenon. Many of the features of anxiety – the racing heart, the widely dilated pupil, the tense muscles – prepare the individual for flight from danger. This concept however does not help us very much when we come to coping with anxiety in everyday life when anxiety, instead of being helpful, becomes crippling. Unfortunately in modern society flight or fight solves few if any of the inner tensions brought about by anxiety. And so to understand its nature it is necessary to look further than the purely biological facts and try to discover why morbid or useless anxiety occurs.

Illustrative Case History

A man of forty-five complained of chronic palpitation and chest pain. The attacks came on at various times of the day and were not related to exercise or to food or to drink. Rarely were symptoms troublesome at night. The pain was described as 'gripping', as though somebody was tightening a band around the chest. Usually the pain lasted a few minutes, but on occasion the palpitation lasted for several hours.

The social history in this case was interesting. The patient started life in a simple way as a travelling salesman. But he had within the last ten years developed wide business interests, and was now the managing director of a large public company. All his life he had been a 'glutton for work', and seldom took a holiday. He confessed to a considerable personal fortune. Nevertheless he felt driven to work harder and harder each year to consolidate his financial future. Married, with two children in their late teens, he described his family life as happy and rewarding.

Physical examination was entirely normal, except for obesity and a poor tolerance of exercise. Because of his chest pain he was referred to a consultant physician, who carried out extensive investigations which included electrocardiography, chest X-ray and barium meal tests. All these investigations showed his health to be quite normal and he was reassured that there was nothing physically wrong. He was advised to lose weight, smoke less and take more exercise. His palpitation and pains were explained as being due to 'nerves'.

For a while the patient's symptoms disappeared. But they returned with greater severity a few weeks later. Now he looked less well, despite a slight loss of weight. He was, however more ready to accept that he was suffering from an anxiety state. It was explained that the attacks of palpitation or racing of the heart are common when people are bedevilled with chronic anxiety. The heart reacts to the production of excess adrenalin by the body in the same way as it does in a really stressful situation. For example, a threat from a foe is met by fighting, or running away, and both need a rapid heart action. The chest pain can often be due to chronic muscle tension, again on the basis of a flight-or-fight situation, in which body muscles are over-alerted and ready for some specific action which, however, never actually materializes.

Throughout the whole of this consultation the patient maintained an air of polite interest tempered with incredulity. Eventually he pointed out that the similes were understood but he could not see the relevance as far as he was concerned. He did not feel threatened, nor was he in a position in which it was necessary to pick a fight or quarrel with anyone. He employed people to fight his battles. He agreed however to try a course of tranquillizers.

This particular patient was lost sight of for a period of just over a year, then he came back with similar symptoms. But now at times the symptoms kept him away from work for days on end. On his own initiative he had consulted another physician and been referred to a psychiatrist who had confirmed the diagnosis of an anxiety state, and prescribed further tranquillizers. The patient, however, still could not understand why he, a man with everything he wanted both for himself and his family, could find his body so upset by nerves. It was decided to try to rationalize this man's life situation for him by means of a fuller exploration of his basic anxiety.

After a long discussion about the nature of anxiety he was eventually able to accept the fact that the fundamental dis-ease of his personality made his body react as if it were exposed to danger. A strong feeling of deprivation was discovered (see Ch. 2). All his life he had subconsciously felt insecure, and much of his drive and ambition had arisen to compensate for this feeling. A sense of inner emptiness haunted him and constantly promoted an anxious desire for possessions. As he became more successful he had had to delegate more and more of his responsibility to his various directors and subordinates. This in a way was 'giving away' prized possessions – giving away things that made him feel secure.

In other words, the psychological bargain he had struck within himself as a young man to compensate for a feeling of basic insecurity was now in danger of being broken. As he got older he saw other men developing within his own organization who might, one day, threaten his position. And so the basic anxiety in his personality, no longer safely bound by the behaviour and activity that neutralized it in the past, became free and erupted into physical symptoms and feelings.

It must be stressed that this simple explanation did not immediately cure the patient. Neither was it received particularly well at the time, for it is difficult to reorientate what one feels about life at the drop of a hat. Nevertheless it enabled this patient to catch a glimpse of his life situation in a way that had not occurred to him before. He could begin to observe himself in a new light and to understand himself a little better too. Eventually he learned to cope with his symptoms and convince himself of what was causing them. In other words real confidence gradually replaced anxiety, and he felt better.

But it must be realized that the simple domestic psychotherapy, which helped in this case and allowed a reasonably intelligent man to overcome his psychiatric disability, is often very time-consuming as far as doctor and patient are concerned. It is rarely possible in general practice for this very reason. In most cases such therapy is the legitimate ground of the specialized psychotherapist, whether he practices as a private individual or as a leader of group discussions in a National Health Service setting. Such specialist therapy is often as necessary to the psychologically crippled person as insulin is to the diabetic.

The object of this exercise is, however, to point out that one way of overcoming disabling anxiety is to accept reality. This often becomes easier if one is honest with oneself as well as with one's fellows.

CHAPTER TWO

The Supposed Deprivations

In Chapter One a cluster of common themes were mentioned that tend to recur when we try to analyse various real-life situations that are accompanied by anxiety. The first of these themes we have already met, a supposed deprivation which eventually creeps into the consciousness as an anxiety severe enough to produce demoralizing physical symptoms. The example given in the illustrative case history was basically a fear of being deprived of possessions or position.

It has been suggested that a relatively harmless and anxiety-preventing device for patients who suffer from this particular feeling of deprivation is collecting for example stamps, *objets d'art*, or even butterflies. Another indication that deprivation of material possessions is affecting someone is a type of behaviour that can be called the squirrel complex, in which the victim finds it almost physically impossible to throw anything away. As a result cupboards, lofts, garages and houses gradually fill up with useless clutter, bric-à-brac and furniture that might well have been discarded years ago.

The interesting thing about these phenomena is that they may prevent episodes of frank anxiety. A flaw has doubtless occurred during the development of the personality, usually at an early stage. But this defect, if you like, has been successfully enough concealed, and the covering up itself has in turn sometimes greatly enhanced the apparent success of the individual in question.

Of course the effect of the supposed deprivations varies from person to person. A useful example is the sense of time deprivation that can spoil much that is pleasant or rewarding in life. A feeling of time deprivation frequently occurs in students, although it can equally well apply to a housewife who suddenly feels she has no time to do anything and succeeds in the end in doing nothing, so painful and absorbing are her anxiety symptoms. Students usually experience time depriation after a period of inactivity, maybe after a long holiday or a period of slackness. Then suddenly the textbooks look enormous. A chapter is hastily read, and because this is done in a state of anxiety and tension, little is taken in – not a difficult state of affairs to understand when one considers for a moment that the body has been physically mobilized for a flight or fight situation and not for the steady mental effort of learning. Anxious panic therefore often follows and examinations are sometimes failed because of this.

Illustrative Case History

A bright student, with several O levels easily attained, was working for a number of A levels, well within her intellectual powers, and a University place had been provisionally secured. Because she found learning easy and had some talent for acting she took on a leading part in the school play, for she was a competent and convincing amateur actress. After the success of her theatrical rôle she found herself a little behind in her work schedules.

The examinations were still several months away, but suddenly she found she could not concentrate and felt she would fail all her tests. She had blinding headaches and complained of eye strain. Full physical examination, including reference to an occulist, disclosed no abnormality. A superficial examination of her past history revealed that she had been adopted at the age of one year by a rather emotionless and ambitious couple. Although at first she made convincing statements about the happiness of her home life, when more closely questioned she admitted that often she felt a need for affection, and wanted to know 'who she was'.

It was suggested that her physical symptoms were mainly reflections of a feeling of 'time deprivation', a common student hazard, and that in her subconscious ideas of being a 'deprived' person as far as affection was concerned had implemented a state of mind which led her into an episode of neurotic illness. After a fair amount of support and encouragement she recommenced her studies – and incidentally achieved the good grades she deserved.

Some students also suffer from this deprivation during an actual examination. These are the candidates who arrive at the examination hall hours in advance to avoid being late. Their writing is often so hurried that it finishes up as a meaningless scrawl and at *viva-voce* tests they mix up their answers and the words tumble out in great confusion. Often they fail examinations that should have been passed easily and are classed as 'poor examinees'. In actual fact, a sense of time deprivation often has them in its grip, and their performance is being upset by painful anxiety, which clouds their thoughts and obscures their judgement.

Escaping from this dilemma can be brought about only by training for confidence in the face of the examination situation. Most examinations are held in a ritualistic atmosphere that can be quite frightening to some people. But confidence may be learned by mock examinations, in which errors in examination technique rather than knowledge may be pointed out to the examinee and countered effectively. Any difference between a student's normal fair round hand and the illegible writing of the over-anxious examinee should be carefully noted by teachers and the matter taken up fully with the scholar – if necessary through the parents and with a doctor. In all probability more good students fail examinations because of anxiety than from any other single cause. Of recent years University health services have seconded trained psychiatrists to help them deal with undergraduates' psychological problems. These services, when available, should be used to the fullest extent.

One of the most interesting things about anxiety, and this is something we will notice time and time again as we explore this world of worry and fear, is the strange way in which we tend to modify our otherwise reasonable behaviour in an attempt to avoid experiencing the personal pain of anxiety. One common method already mentioned is to cover up anxious feelings with aggressive behaviour. I don't think there is any doubt that much wild, aggressive and dangerous driving can be explained in this way. Particularly when an episode of extraordinary aggressiveness suddenly erupts in an otherwise calm, conscientious and very competent driver.

Illustrative Case

On the way to my consulting rooms I have to negotiate a series of sharp corners and bends in a winding lane. All the way there is plenty of room for a car going in each direction, provided both vehicles keep well to their side of the road. One winter's evening I was driving carefully down this road in a borrowed car – my own was at the service station – when I saw a neighbour of mine approaching in his car. He was well over to my side of the road and coming towards me quite fast. I pulled in well to the left, the tyres grazing the side of the road as I did so, and by great good luck there was no collision.

We both stopped, and then I was amazed to hear the driver of the other car hurling abuse at me through the wound-down window before driving off again, obviously in a great fury. Because lighting conditions were poor and I was driving a car unknown to him, my neighbour, whom I had always known as a charming man and who incidentally was usually a very careful driver, did not recognize me.

Later I heard from his wife that at the time of the incident he had been under great strain, his firm having been taken over by a larger company. He had been 'run off his feet', she said, and 'hardly knew which way he was going'. It seems likely in this case that distressing feelings of anxiety made him belligerent and stemmed from an experience of time deprivation. It erupted as an episode of extreme aggressiveness quite out of character with his normal behaviour.

Anyone who sees the driving behaviour of those who have very tight time schedules to keep – for example drivers for private delivery firms who are by the nature of their work very much at the mercy of the clock, cannot fail to notice their aggressive and competitive behaviour on the road. This contrasts with the unhurried care and professionalism of the long-distance lorry driver, whose day is clearly more orderly and less stress-ridden.

Another very common type of anxiety that cuts unkindly into many people's experience of living is a feeling of sleep deprivation. In recent years, due to facts gained in 'sleep laboratories' in this country and in the US, the whole subject of sleep and sleep deprivation has been put on to a scientific footing. The sleeping habits of hundreds of patients, good sleepers and self-confessed insomniacs have been studied in great detail, and one of the interesting facts to come to light as a result of these experiments has been the explosion of the fallacy that insomnia, unless it is artificially enforced, has a deleterious effect on health. What is more, many of the statements made by insomniacs as to the amount of time they actually sleep each night are extremely inaccurate.

Many of the symptoms that insomniacs actually suffer are in fact anxiety symptoms, stemming not from lack of sleep but from a supposed deprivation of sleep.

Illustrative Case History

The patient was a conscientious middle-aged widow who held a responsible job in the Civil Service. She appeared very tense and worried and complained that she had been in the habit of taking barbiturate sleeping pills regularly for the last ten years, and had eventually reached the stage where unless she took 600 mgs of sodium amytal – a very high dosage – each night she did not sleep properly. When asked what she meant by 'sleep properly' she explained that she would take ages to go to sleep, would hear the local clocks chiming all through the night and felt, on waking, unable to face her demanding job. It was pointed out that possibly her symptoms had nothing to do with insomnia, but were due to a feeling of sleep deprivation, and that no one has ever come to any physical or mental harm because of insomnia. We all, in fact, get the amount of sleep we need.

It was also explained that her regular dose of barbiturate was exceedingly high. She would need to reduce it gradually and replace it, for the time being, with another hypnotic. She was very reluctant to take this advice, especially when she was told that she would 'sleep badly' while undergoing the treatment. Eventually she agreed to try the experiment of gradually withdrawing barbiturate drugs during a holiday period. At last she learned the 'trick' of sleeping without drugs.

This and many similar cases of sleep deprivation anxiety are complicated by the phenomenon that is becoming known as dream-deprivation neurosis. Recent work has shown that each of us has a normal dream rhythm, the regular periodicity of which is extremely necessary for our mental health and well-being. If a person is artificially deprived of his dream sequences during sleep he develops symptoms of agitation, nervousness and sometimes depression.

Experimental methods exist for waking a patient during periods of dreaming. Dreams can also be monitored quite easily by means of simple electrical devices. It has been proved, without doubt, that barbiturate-induced sleep suppresses normal dreaming, and so the barbiturate-addicted insomniac has a double load of psychological trouble to carry – a physically-induced complex of drug symptoms plus, frequently, a component of supposed sleep deprivation anxiety.

Perhaps an even more far-reaching cause of anxiety is brought about by contact deprivation which is demonstrated by the experience of simple loneliness. The intensely miserable feelings of loneliness have been very well chronicled ever since man first expressed himself by the written word. Before this songs and ballads described loneliness, and enumerated the effects it had on the human being. Even today many of the specially successful popular songs are ones dealing with the despair of loneliness and the anxiety that clings to it fundamentally. That anxiety symptoms can erupt purely and simply as a result of contact deprivation in the modern world has, however, recently been shown in settings far removed from art or literature. For example, it can occur in the inhabitants of a council estate, not isolated in the depths of the country but within a few miles of central London.

A well-documented example of this contact deprivation was a study made by two medical investigators, Taylor and Chave, in a community situated in rural Hertfordshire. Near a main railway line, less than three-quarters of an hour from the West End of London, shortly after the end of the Second World War, were housed families who had previously been living in extremely poor conditions in London. They had been rehoused in pleasant dwellings built on land which had comprised part of a millionaire's estate and an exclusive North London golf course.

The general practitioners who looked after this community found a startlingly high incidence of neurosis in these people compared with people in the rest of the country, and a special investigation carried out on this estate and other similarly sited ones showed patterns of behaviour that were highly characteristic of anxiety. Contact deprivation, although the inhabitants were often less than the width of a brick away from one another, generated this highly specialized anxiety.

Because of difficulties in obtaining supplies of raw materials for building at this post-war period it was official policy to erect all the dwelling houses before shops, cafés, public houses or churches. This meant that all the traditional points of contact within a community were absent. The residents, uprooted from their overcrowded, unhealthy and often insanitary previous environment, therefore experienced a short and sharp attack of contact deprivation anxiety, which was to spoil the lives of some for several years. Now, about ten years later, all the normal points of human contact have been successfully provided and the incidence of anxiety reactions in this community is level with that in the rest of Britain. It is to be hoped that future planners will take psychological as well as economic factors into consideration before they begin building for new communities.

Many of the particular anxiety reactions in old people stem likewise from a sense of contact deprivation, often secondary to an increasing immobility and lessening of sensory contact with the world. Deafness and poor vision are quite often the main cause for this loss of contact with others. Of course we all have to face in advancing years some contraction in our experience of the environment. But all too often a supposed contact deprivation is superadded to the real situation, and this is extremely liable to lead to anxiety symptoms.

There is little doubt that women are, in a general sense, very much more robust than men. Their expectation of life is longer and they are capable of bearing considerably greater physical strains than men. Nevertheless they consult their doctors more frequently than men do, and a large number of these consultations are for episodes of neurotic illness, including anxiety states.

There have been many reasons postulated to account for this curious phenomenon. Hormones, easier accessibility to the doctor and many other factors have all been put forward to explain this curious paradox in which the more sturdy and healthy sex seem to need the doctor's attentions so frequently. Perhaps, however, the solution is quite simple. There seems little reason for men to have either more or less anxiety in everyday life than women do. Menfolk, however, build up an anti-anxiety factor as a happy result of their various group activities.

Women have often been referred to as the unclubbable sex, and although there is a variety of group activities that are essentially female, compared with menfolk women lead relatively isolated lives even when they are involved in work outside the home. Men, however, whether married or single, tend to enjoy a fairly tightly integrated group life. Large towns and cities nearly always contain several exclusively male clubs, and there are of course thousands of organizations up and down the country catering largely for male patronage. In a public house or a bar it is unusual to see a *solitary* man taking refreshment, and of course half the attraction of the 'local' stems from its clublike atmosphere.

The following short case history is a good illustration of 'the unclubbable sex', showing the social and medical hazards which confront it.

Illustrative Case History

An elderly woman left London to come and reside near her son in a semi-countrified suburb. He lived only five minutes' walk away, and both he and his wife visited his mother regularly. They looked after her when she was unwell and supported her during periods of bad weather. Nevertheless her general psychological condition deteriorated and this was reflected in her loss of pride in looking after her small bungalow. The garden rapidly became untidy, the windows were never cleaned, the door knocker lost its gleam of polish, and the muddle in the rooms mounted every day.

Physical symptoms of anxiety became obvious in the patient and included palpitation, complaints of excessive sweating, twitching of the legs and a tremor of the hands. When she was encouraged to talk about herself she said that life had suddenly lost its meaning. She was sure it had been a mistake to move from her own town home, and that now, even though her son and daughter-in-law were close by, she had no real friends. She felt life was unkind, and her body reacted to its 'unkindness' by the production of symptoms that gave her a justifiable excuse for further depriving herself of life's pleasures.

It was often suggested to her that her behaviour was not in her own interests, and that from the point of view of comfort she was far better off now than she had been in her previous home. Eventually it was agreed that she should return to London to stay with a relative for perhaps three months, so that she could compare the advantages and disadvantages of the two environments. Long before the agreed period had elapsed she returned to her bungalow.

Then at last by her own efforts, together with the strong support of her son and the local social services, her state of mind began to improve. Returning to the real situation of her previous existence had demonstrated to her far more effectively than words could the extent to which she had clouded the 'real' deprivations she was experiencing as a result of her move with apparent ones she had supposed to exist.

> When forty winters shall beseige thy brow,
> And dig deep trenches in thy beauty's field,
> Thy youth's proud livery, so gaz'd on now,
> Will be a tatter'd weed, of small worth held.

The opening words of one of Shakespeare's sonnets express with characteristic economy the poet's attitude to the changing face of women as the years pass by, and it is not surprising that what a woman sees, or thinks she sees, in the mirror affects her state of mind.

Illustrative Case History

A good-looking and intelligent woman, who appeared rather younger than her forty-five years, complained of being constantly strung up, tense and anxious. Her husband was a member of the *Institute of Directors* which extends their routine medical examination scheme to the wives of its members, and she had had repeated physical checks, all of which proved that her health was normal. On examination she was observed to have many of the classical physical symptoms of anxiety. To start with it was difficult to pin down what was triggering off her particular symptoms. There were no menopausal troubles, but during the process of giving a full medical history she came out spontaneously with the statement that she had always dreaded entering her middle-forties. This was the time she assumed that all women 'fell to pieces', lost their looks and 'started to sprout hair on their faces'.

She was so obviously convinced of this that it was suggested to her that much of what she felt was wrong with her body sprang from a fear of image deprivation. Part of her everyday life had been a routine, elaborate 'facial' each morning, and it was possible to relate her anxiety mostly to periods just after this routine which recently had become an exercise in hunting for signs of an approaching loss of looks. The hypothesis was put to her that subconscious feelings of deprivation can produce anxiety from the age of the cradle onwards. A sense of deprivation was making her anxious because the face that looked back at her from the mirror was not as young-looking and beautiful as it once had been. Her body image had 'slipped' as it were.

It was suggested to her that there is no particular age at which a woman loses her looks, and that every stage of living has its own beauty, provided excess nervous tension and worry over the ever-changing self are not excessive. A break in her introspection was advocated.

With this patient, as with all cases in which simple domestic psychotherapy is practised, it was necessary to delve fairly deeply and at length into the various ways in which anxiety had affected the human soul. This allowed her to gradually accept that the very real physical symptoms she was experiencing actually sprang from her unconscious mind. Once this hurdle was cleared she was advised to analyse her way of life in the light of her new knowledge. Eventually she found she could turn her active brain to more rewarding subjects and her anxiety gradually became less troublesome.

Love deprivation is a subject of enormous interest to certain Freudian psychiatrists. But unfortunately much of the theory of this interesting school of psychoanalysis has been misunderstood by the layman, or rejected as being absurd or incredible. Nevertheless, feelings of love deprivation in a patient can generate anxiety incredibly easily.

Illustrative Case History

A girl was brought for examination by her mother because she appeared to be a compulsive eater. Although she was only seventeen and five feet four inches tall she already weighed over thirteen stone and had an insatiable appetite for fattening carbohydrate foods. The girl's father had died of cancer two years previously and had been missed very severely by the whole family, but specially by this, his only daughter. In recent months the mother had been courted by another man and was preparing to marry him.

On examination the patient was generally awkward and difficult to engage in conversation. Her finger nails were severely bitten and she had a resentful and anxious expression. Recently she had refused to go to school because everyone made fun of her, and she spent a lot of time moping about in her bedroom.

Physical examination produced entirely negative results except for the presence of the classical signs of tension and anxiety. It was explained separately to the patient and her mother that her overeating pattern was simply brought about by a supposed deprivation of love. Having already lost one parent through death she saw herself losing the other one through remarriage. Her feeling of supposed deprivation of familial love was reflected subconsciously in a need for oral comfort, and she was attempting to comfort herself and to escape her painful feelings of anxiety by eating. This particular girl needed a considerable amount of support in a group situation at a psychiatric hospital, and a very special effort on the part of her mother and the intended husband, before her anxiety was allayed sufficiently to allow her to settle down to a sensible diet and begin to lose weight. To have attempted weight reduction in her previously disturbed state of mind would have made her very much worse.

Of course examples of compensation of this sort are not in any way limited to teenagers. They are constantly seen when someone is 'overlooked', perhaps when promotion to a better job is expected, or when a candidate is rejected in an application for a job. In the latter situation the reasons for not being chosen are seldom known to the applicant, and are often not explicable in any logical way that he can understand. Indeed in many cases they boil down to something quite unrelated to his true worth.

When many candidates apply for a much-sought-after position all holding equal 'paper' qualifications the success of one or the other may depend on such matters as the cut of a suit or the pitch of a voice. All too often, however, an unsuccessful applicant feels acutely anxious after such a rejection, and much of his anxiety results from the unconscious supposition that he is unloved, or rather valued lower than his true worth. If, happily, he obtains the next post for which he applies, these subconscious feelings soon evaporate. Repeated failures, however, are known to precipitate anxiety states.

Illustrative Case History

A man aged forty was seen after he had failed a life assurance examination. He was considerably overweight and had a raised blood pressure and very poor tolerance to exercise. He was also tense and worried and it seemed likely that both his physical and psychological abnormalities had a common cause. A detailed personal history confirmed this.

About a year previously he had lost his position, that of a sales director in an old family business, as the result of a takeover bid. He had obtained a fair redundancy payment and was well thought of in his own professional world, and it did not strike him for a moment that he would have any trouble in finding further suitable employment.

Unhappily, however, although he was short-listed for various posts, he was not successful in obtaining the sort of job he expected. Around this time he started to put on a great deal of weight–and to a certain extent this was due to excessive drinking brought about, in all probability, as a result of his personal anxiety about the future. Although he at last obtained a promising position which was superannuable once again he failed the medical due to hypertension and obesity.

This patient found it extremely difficult to face up to the fact that anxiety was making him ill, and that physical causes were not accounting for his high blood pressure. It was put to him that a good investment as far as his health was concerned would be a period of psychotherapy. After a certain amount of persuasion the patient agreed, and the services of an analyst were obtained. Eventually, after several months of treatment he was fit enough, psychologically and physically, to obtain a reasonably responsible post. Perhaps if I had had at that time a fuller appreciation of the nature of anxiety, I would have been able to help this patient understand his own fears more reasonably.

For women the menopause is the main time of life for anxiety reactions, and they frequently compensate by vicarious overeating with the result that they tend to become obese. Once again the eating forms a substitute comfort to mitigate against painful, subjective aspects of the anxiety generated within them by yet another modification of the supposed deprivation state.

Secretly many women believe that when the change of life occurs it will undoubtedly be a change for the worse. Life's pleasures are passing, and the rest of the world will be a dull, grey place for them. To some extent their subsequent misery is relieved if they compensate at the table, and obtain oral gratification for the supposed deprivation which hovers over them like the sword of Damocles. Sometimes, because of medical pressures, or even the dictates of fashion, they muster enough willpower to adhere to the rigours of a strict diet, and all too frequently frank anxiety of a classic nature then erupts and brings them to a doctor.

Illustrative Case History

A woman of forty-six whose periods had been irregular for eighteen months suddenly started getting attacks of panic in the middle of the night. She would wake up panting and was extremely frightened and apprehensive. She also complained of indigestion, with constant burping and attacks of intermittent looseness of the bowels. Sometimes during the day she would suddenly feel her chest so constricted that she could not breathe, and felt she had to pant for air. At other times she would feel sweaty, get tingling of the limbs, and fear she was going to collapse. Physical examination, including blood-pressure estimation, intestinal X-ray and cardiac tests, showed no abnormality. She was, however, nearly two stone overweight. It was suggested to her and to her husband (who was also extremely anxious over her health), that her symptoms were a manifestation of an anxiety state, and that perhaps the menopause was the precipitating factor.

At a later date, and after a certain amount of sedation, the patient felt able to ask simple questions about the menopause. Apparently she and her husband had always enjoyed a very full and satisfactory sex relationship. She feared this would soon come to an end. In other words, she had anticipated a deprivation in this important corner of her life.

A simple explanation about the facts of the matter went a long way towards dispelling her erroneous supposition. She was told that many couples enjoy their normal sex life well on into later years. At first she thought this was merely an example of reassurance, unsupported by facts, but when the results of several surveys on the subject were put before her she became convinced and gradually her symptoms settled down.

Experience has frequently demonstrated to me that feelings of deprivation are often at the root of anxiety symptoms of a puzzling nature. Fairly well rooted in most people's minds is a fear of operations. Now from the logical point of view most operations are extremely safe procedures, and probably far safer than, for example, many commonplace sports and pastimes happily risked by the average man and woman.

But to most people, simply to show statistics of safety does not dispel their innate and basic anxiety about surgical operations. One patient gave me a clue as to how a feeling of being deprived of some of her body substance generated the anxiety she felt about dental treatment. She stated spontaneously that it was not having the injection or the actual dental extraction that worried her, but simply the loss of the tooth. She was going to be altered. Her subconscious feelings of body deprivation generated anxiety.

Patients undergoing surgery often, I am sure, subconsciously resent the loss of an organ, even if the offending structure is diseased and non-functional. Akin to this is the anxiety of women who suffer from excessively heavy periods (menorrhagia). Although repeated estimations of the haemoglobin content of the blood show that the occasional excessive blood loss they are experiencing is not affecting their health in any way, they complain of feeling 'wrung out', tense, tired and worried. In many cases psychological factors are causing these feelings. They are really suffering from supposed deprivation of a vital body fluid.

Sometimes gynaecologists are persuaded to remove the womb in such a patient, so great is her anxiety about the repeated menstrual loss. Unfortunately in such cases this often makes matters worse, as anxiety is given fresh stimulus by a deprivation in yet another vital part.

Asthma is known to be a disease in which the attacks of wheeziness are precipitated by anxiety. Although the real nature of asthma is still largely not understood, suppositions about the suitability of certain airs and climates which preoccupy many asthmatics are related to feelings of being deprived of the 'proper, good, clean and suitable air' which they feel is their birthright. These feelings of being deprived are often expressed by asthmatic patients in their constant search for the climate or place that 'agrees' with them or, for that matter, their children. It is also expressed by the compulsive throwing open of all the windows in the house when an asthmatic attack occurs or is threatened.

A little earlier an example was given that illustrated how a supposed deprivation of love gave rise to painful feelings that were compensated for by excessive eating, and when the eating was restricted frank anxiety would erupt. This sort of compensating mechanism is also seen in more sophisticated situations. Sometimes the feeling of supposed deprivation is so upsetting that the person adopts a *real* deprivation to mask it, or take its place.

One of the aspects of certain neurotic individuals which appears most baffling is the way they involve themselves in difficult situations that would tax the mental strength of even the most psychologically robust. An intriguing facet of this behaviour is a tendency for those who have supposed deprivations, and who subsequently suffer from anxiety as a result to put themselves into situations in which real deprivation faces them.

Illustrative Case History

A young man had led an anxiety-ridden youth, largely as a result of feelings of love deprivation. His parents were both successful doctors, and although they had only limited time at their disposal to look after their son, they were for the most part kind and reasonable people. The boy obviously compared himself with acquaintances and friends who appeared to get more attention from their fathers and mothers, who spent a greater proportion of their time and energy looking after their children.

Although to some extent it was possible to help this patient by frank discussion of the various problems involved in the genesis of anxiety, domestic psychotherapy was far from curative and in the course of time he came to know and eventually married a girl whose emotional background had been extremely traumatic. Her father was an alcoholic and her mother a cold, frigid and embittered woman, who believed all men were fundamentally evil and that everything pertaining to sex was a sin. It is not surprising that the daughter grew up to be a scheming, emotionally barren young woman, who immediately realized how lucky she was to have met an eligible young man who appeared to be in love with her.

In all probability he was attracted to her primarily because of her real deprivations. It was obvious to the patient, even before marriage, that her paucity of real emotion would put him in the position of a husband who would suffer from real deprivations and bad luck, and who could therefore legitimately be pitied by the world.

The temptation to overide his (neurotic) feelings of supposed deprivation with an appraisal of the real situation was too great for him. Needless to say a union based on such insecure foundations was far from happy and soon foundered.

So far we have examined one cardinal causative factor in the genesis of anxiety: a (false) feeling of deprivation which is multilateral in the ways in which it can affect our way of life and our relationship with others. In the next chapter we look at another common cause for chronic anxiety – the 'supposed inexplicables'.

CHAPTER THREE

The Supposed Inexplicables

The relationship of anxiety to fear is an intimate one. 'I'm anxious', and 'I'm afraid', are in many ways expressions of a similar feeling. But the fundamental difference between them is wide and pertinent if we are to try to understand how anxiety arises in everyday life.

Fear is a basic emotion. Knowing when to be afraid and perhaps run away is often necessary for survival. But to be afraid predisposes a known object and a known danger. Freud put forward the suggestion that a fear of unknown dangers is the essence of what is experienced in neurotic anxiety. But even well adjusted, unneurotic people often experience anxiety when they become involved with fears they cannot master or explain. This is the *vague threat* that may hang over us, a fear of the unknown, the inexplicable.

A threat like this is intangible. There is so much of a nothingness in it that usually it is impossible for us to meet it in the same way as we can meet other 'threats', either with courage or by intelligent flight. And so it tends to hover over us generating all the classical symptoms of anxiety we have read about in the previous chapters.

The basic power of the inexplicable as a factor in the production of anxiety has been appreciated far more by writers and poets than by doctors. In the Greek legend of Perseus and the Gorgons a good and ancient example of the situation occurs. It will be remembered that by using the reflecting qualities of Athena's shield, Perseus averted his eyes from the glare of the baleful Medusa, and in this way he could cut off her head quite safely, for he avoided the 'inexplicable' hazard that was involved – that of being turned to stone on the spot by her glance. The feeling of being 'frozen to the spot' is common in those who suddenly come face to face with a totally inexplicable and potent anxiety-producing situation.

Similar devices to escape feared and incomprehensible influences crop up frequently in modern life. The *jettura,* with his *malochio* or 'evil eye', is a source of great anxiety to the inhabitants of certain parts of Southern Italy even today. Escape from his influence is mainly brought about by deflecting the evil glance by means of a curious selection of jewellery, charms or trinkets. Many of the rites of modern savages, in remote areas of the world, are mainly directed towards allaying the 'inexplicable' powers of demons or deities.

The horrific anxiety-producing effects of the unknown were well appreciated, of course, by the classic poets. Shakespeare demonstrated this admirably when Hamlet tosses aside the 'consummation devoutly to be wished', which would bring an end to the 'heartache, and the thousand shocks' that his 'flesh is heir to', mainly because of the anxious reaction that leapt into his mind as he thought, 'What dreams may come when we have shuffled off this mortal coil?' The terror of the (inexplicable) possibility of dreaming, when in the state of nothingness (i.e. death), was too much for him to contemplate. The uncanniness of death, in many ways the ultimate when we come to consider the 'supposed inexplicables' in conjunction with anxiety, is closely related to a fear of a state of nothingness. Anxiety-producing situations of a more commonplace nature crop up frequently in life, where unaccountable fears seem to be implicated.

Illustrative Case History

Years ago the author was walking over some remote countryside in North Wales when he came across a deserted village at the head of a small valley. The day was fine and sunny, and the glassless windows of the empty cottages moved gently in a slight breeze. Although there was nothing in the scene to suggest anything of a sinister nature, quite suddenly a strong feeling of anxiety was experienced, accompanied by intense sweating and palpitation. To one side of the road was a ruined stone-works where much of the machinery had been left intact, and a large trimming saw had cut half-way through a large piece of slate. It was characteristic of a place where, it seemed, the people had unaccountably left their homes, perhaps because of unexpected and fearful disaster. Further down the valley fields and lakes were very beautiful, but the whole day was overshadowed by a vague and unreasoning feeling of anxiety that was slow to evaporate.

All of us have experiences of this type from time to time. Always they are completely irrational, and in this case the anxiety produced suggests that a phobic element was attached to deserted areas and situations. As we shall see, mild phobic fears do provide, in many cases, a tolerable way of mopping up free-floating anxieties in the mind.

Such devices are, of course, quite unconscious, and unconscious mechanisms for escaping the terrors of anxiety are extremely common.

One of the most interesting aspects of human behaviour today is a vast preoccupation with the bizarre or horrific. Novels and television plays, the cinema and the theatre are geared to give ample opportunity for indulging this whim of human nature. Almost any theatre production or book that contains a fair quotient of horror – be it monsters from outer space, Frankenstein variations or merely frank horrific brutality – seems sure of a large and fairly ready appreciation. It is striking how often timid folk, who at face value one would think happier with gentler entertainment, devote themselves to this sort of theme.

There is little doubt that we all have a fairly constant quota of inherent anxiety in our make-up, and as was stressed in the

Introduction, this anxiety is quite necessary in many cases, for it helps us to achieve legitimate goals and pursue our ultimate aims in life. It seems likely that real and potentially damaging anxiety is, however, rather different to this 'drive' anxiety, and many of its painful terrors may be warded off by exploiting these vicarious 'thrill' situations. Their value lies in being able to soak up real anxiety, like blotting paper does ink.

This is probably the reason why physical freaks, deformities or horrors, strange and weird or puzzling situations somehow tend to hold our interest, in many cases against our better (conscious) judgement. A variation on this theme is seen in certain fields of entertainment which involve health matters. Television programmes dealing with operations and the more spectacular feats of surgery today always draw large audiences, and it may be that anxiety concerning a possible operation that *may be* lurking round the corner for us explains why we view with such fascination the application of surgery to others. The picture on our television screen is an image that happily excludes the reality factor. It makes us mildly anxious, but we know that to escape this anxiety all we have to do is to switch over to another channel and so we can bear to watch.

Getting rid of the anxiety related to supposed inexplicables is not as easy as allaying the symptoms brought to the surface when we are dealing with supposed deprivations. And the reason for this is possibly that the more inaccessible and inner reaches of the personality are involved in this sort of anxiety. Nevertheless, various psychic mechanisms have developed that can help us in this way, and these are worth examining in a little detail. The tendency to *bind* anxiety to certain specific situations, as in a phobia, has previously been mentioned. Phobias are extremely common, and many people have phobic fears of one sort or another. In phobic states it is not a real situation which is upsetting the nervous system – this is demonstrated in the simple case of a fear of heights. Many people suffer from dizziness, giddiness, trembling and other physical symptoms of anxiety when they are six feet up in the air on a stepladder. But they are unlikely to be affected in this way when at a height of thousands of feet in an aircraft. In other words, height as such is not the real cause of their phobic fear. It originates in the subconscious mind, and probably a phobia about heights, cats, spiders or what you will, allows the person involved to live a perfectly normal life, not overruled by damaging anxiety, provided they avoid their particular *bête noir*.

Sometimes however a phobic fear can expand its effects and become psychologically crippling, and this is when medical aid is needed.

Illustrative Case History

The patient was in late middle age and since his wife, of whom he had never been very fond, died, had gone to live with his elderly mother. Although he admitted to being a nervous person he managed to remain well enough while the mother was alive. Eventually she died too, and fairly quickly the patient started to experience severe anxiety symptoms. These occurred only when he left his house and when questioned about the nature of his fears all he could do was to repeat that he had a vague dread of something terrible happening to him while he was out in the road, shopping or going to work. Despite psychotherapy at a hospital and heavy daytime and night sedation his symptoms did not improve.

At last his private hell of agoraphobia (literally, fear of the market place) became so acute that he gave up a good job to live entirely within the environment of his home, his material needs being brought to his door by either neighbours or tradesmen. As long as he kept within this environment he escaped anxiety, but the payment exacted by the phobia – that safety-bound his free-floating anxiety and kept him reasonably happy – was excessively high. In the light of modern knowledge little can be done to cure such patients. This particular man gained a little strength by coming to terms with his fear and accepting it as a part of his life. A psychotherapist would probably be able to trace this sort of disability to a basic breakdown of personality maturation. The patient probably failed to develop emotionally very much after adolescence. His anxiety may well have been centred around the necessity of leaving his home and mother to make his mark in the world, which he found inexplicable and frightening.

Another device used by the unconscious for 'turning away' anxiety is now graced with the term *blocking*. This can occur in various forms, the most primitive of which is the vaso-vagal syndrome, or in other words, the fainting attack. The medical student who faints at his first operating session is escaping from the intolerable wave of anxiety that has broken over him at the violation of what has previously been one of nature's taboos – that is, that blood should not be shed. When an 'inexplicable' situation is suddenly handed to him, i.e. that blood can be shed, and is being shed at this very minute, he escapes from it psychologically by loss of consciousness. Of course in Victorian times escaping anxiety-prone situations by this method was common, and it has been asserted that a poorly toned vascular system together with the evils of tight lacing in the Victorian young lady made swooning more prevalent than it is today. This is perhaps an interesting illustration of how the physical and psychological can interact to cause a pattern of behaviour.

A more sophisticated form of blocking which provides escape from anxiety is a sub-conscious turning away from a potentially worrying situation, and many people rationalize their anxious fears in this way. For example, there can be no doubt that the chance of dying of cancer of the lung is increased proportionately by day-to-day cigarette consumption. The fact that so many people still smoke cigarettes can only be explained by supposing that the anxiety which might be generated at the thought of dying a relatively slow and unpleasant death is blocked by a subconscious turning away from the situation.

These package deals all of us make with reality often feature in psychic escape mechanisms. But they do tend to break down rather rapidly if the *unreal* in our personal experience suddenly becomes very real. For example, if a near or dear friend loses his health or life through cancer due to smoking, frank anxiety about our own smoking habits erupts.

Another way in which the anxiety of a painful nature is sometimes dealt with automatically is known technically as *conversion*. Sometimes this converts anxiety into a simple bodily symptom, such as palpitation or breathlessness, or at other times loss of function of perhaps a limb or one of the special senses. Conversion symptoms are particularly common when anxiety springs from 'inexplicable' sources.

Illustrative Case History

A young pilot with a distinguished operational record who had been decorated for gallantry during the war was seen at a medical board because of frequent and disabling migrainous headaches. These were associated with a transient but potentially dangerous loss of vision and were clearly a bar to any further flying. Now although this young man loved the air, and had earned a distinguished war record and showed no signs of combat or battle fatigue (he had, in fact, recently volunteered for a hazardous aircrew operation), during his examination at the medical board he admitted that he would not mind having a period out of the pilot's cockpit.

Recently, the aircraft he used to fly so well had been replaced by a more modern and faster machine and there had, unfortunately, been a series of unaccountable crashes involving the prototypes of these aircraft. The chance remark that he felt the teething troubles on this new type of aircraft would be 'ironed out' during the time he was unfit for pilot duty gave an inkling that anxiety concerning the unexplained troubles of the new aircraft was responsible for the pilot's migraine headaches, by means of an unconscious psychic conversion device.

More florid types of conversion symptoms, not always produced by anxiety but triggered off by an inexplicable situation, include a large number of disabilities grouped together under the rather unkind umbrella heading of hysteria. In many cases the hysterical symptom is so closely matched to the apparent medical disability that almost anyone can see the connection: for instance, the amateur singer who loses her voice before the concert she is too anxious to give; the golfer whose back gives out during a trying competitive tournament; or the soldier who can do just about everything except march on a parade, or carry a gun. In most cases hysterical behaviour is comparatively easy to understand, and often it is quite easy to cure, suggestion being all that is necessary in many instances.

The anxiety arising from 'inexplicable' happenings of old age, pain and death, however, provides the doctor with one of his most difficult problems, and the way in which he helps his patients to cope with this anxiety is to some extent a measure of his professional aptitude and success. In this field success lies largely in the prevention of *anticipated* pain and *anticipated* disability in old age.

Experiments have shown quite recently that the level of anxiety experienced by patients is heightened tremendously when it is felt that a situation has passed out of control, and when inexplicable things are happening.

Illustrative Case History

(Taken from *Archiv. of Gen. Psychiatry,* Vol. 15, 6.12.66).

A group of patients, aged between eighteen and forty-nine, who were attending a psychiatric outpatients clinic at the Institute of Psychosomatic and Psychiatric Research and Training Hospital of Chicago, were asked to spend a full day at the hospital. No seriously ill patients were involved in the study, nor was anyone who had recently been suffering from a psychosomatic illness included.

During the morning hours of the experiment, psychological testing was performed and the subjects were brought into the laboratory and familiarized with what was to be for them a test situation. Electrical machines for recording blood pressure, heart rate and so on were attached to various parts of their anatomy by a 'friendly and reassuring' technician. When all was in readiness the 'chief' of the laboratory entered and ceremoniously checked all the equipment. Then after reassuring the patients that all was well he switched on a dummy complex of electronic devices that was clearly visible at the foot of each bed. Finally he told the subjects to be still and relax. The experiment had begun.

After about fifteen minutes noises of a certain and constant character were transmitted through head phones that the patients wore, and the physical reactions were monitored. Then an unexpected anxiety-provoking procedure began. A mild electric shock was administered to everyone and various electrical noises were transmitted by a hidden loudspeaker. The chief rushed in and indicated that something of an inexplicable nature had happened. When complaints were made about the shocks he told the patients to be very still as there 'was a lot of high voltage' about. Almost immediately more 'trouble', in the form of small electrical spark discharges, accompanied by the smell of burning rubber, issued from the dummy apparatus. The chief then 'reassured the subjects in a manner indicating that he was far from sure of the validity of the reassurances'.

Eventually the experiment was concluded by the chief leaving the laboratory to 'cut off the current at a master switch'. Leaving aside the questionable ethics involved in carrying out such tests on patients, judged as 'extremely successful in creating a frightening situation, in which subjects sighed, moaned, groaned and offered desperate advice about corrective measures and pleaded in quavering voices', there seems no doubt that the quality and quantity of the anxiety generated came from the inexplicable nature of what was happening to them. The unknown factor in the situation predominated. Nobody knew what was to follow – more electric shocks, perhaps fire, personal injury or even death by electrocution.

The unknown fears of the elderly, the disabled, or those facing death, and the anxiety they generate, may not be as acute as in this false experimental situation. But they are near enough to it to encourage those who must deal with people in this plight to do their utmost to mitigate against personal anxious agony. In many cases truth and straightforward friendliness are quite the most effective weapons at our disposal when bringing anxious, elderly or dying patients or even relatives, into a state of mind where they can come to terms to some extent with their 'inexplicable' fears. The quiet reassurance that their doctors and nurses have handled patients just like themselves before is often of the greatest value.

CHAPTER FOUR

Anxiety and Lack of Creativity

Until now we have considered two major ways in which natural, protective, or if you prefer it alerting anxiety can be changed and distorted so that it begins first of all to spoil certain aspects of everyday life, and finally in many cases to ruin the whole pleasure of living. Two suppositions are put forward by the unconscious mind and are interpreted by the part of the personality that deals with reason in a way that differs from normal. The supposition that inexplicable forces are at work upon us and we cannot escape their machinations seems to be an altered fear reaction. The other supposition, that we are being deprived for various reasons of that which should be our birthright, can be looked upon perhaps as a modified infantile reaction.

But this is not the end of the story, and there are other feelings stemming from the unconscious that spill over in the conscious mind, and result in the genesis of intolerable anxiety. One is a feeling of being frustrated in a very special way that can be summarized by saying that the victim becomes suddenly aware of a lack of creativity–a frustration, if you like of the basic driving force in life.

Sometimes the etymology of words gives us an unexpected insight into both their true meaning and the basic thoughts and feelings that lie behind them. Anxiety really stems from *angere*, and *anxus* which means to throttle. In other words there is a link between being throttled, or rather shall we say, having one's natural creativity drives throttled or obstructed, and the feeling that we admit to as anxiety. The throttling of life's basic drives and emotions is always associated with feelings of tension and discomfort. This can reach a crippling level, and the individual becomes physically and emotionally tense, anxious and disorganized in his reactions.

The world of simple biology can provide an example as to how this rather sophisticated neurophysiological process has evolved. A simple creature like the unicellular amoeba apparently has no way of coping with noxious stimuli other than by withdrawal, or by entering into a non-active, encysted stage. But as life becomes more complex, with animals containing several cells, special parts of the organism develop which can sample new environmental situations and by feeling them, tasting them or measuring their temperature feed back information to the organism as a whole as to whether or not its life energies can profitably be directed along a certain line. Conversely, these special sense cells can signal whether or not exploration will be hazardous or even dangerous. Once a nervous system develops and a central nervous system, or brain, is present, special sense organs become extremely valuable to the individual. But once a brain has evolved frustration of action is clearly possible, perhaps due to misinformation or conflicting information fed back to it by sense organs, and this can generate anxiety.

Many experimental situations that have been explored demonstrate this state of affairs. For instance a laboratory animal, perhaps a monkey, can learn that by manipulating certain controls in a special way he can receive as a reward a ration of food. In other words, by means of various simple neuromuscular reflexes he finds he can 'create' food, and give himself the subsequent pleasure of eating it. Once this sort of conditioned reflex is firmly established, further experimental modifications in the routine can be made so that on occasion, instead of getting the expected food, an electric shock or some inedible or unacceptable foodstuff is received. This situation first of all tends to generate rage in the animal, and if the experiment is persisted in, anxiety becomes manifest and the animal will resort to any available comforting situation, and perhaps even cuddle up to a warm hot water bottle or a rag doll which he sees as a protective 'mother' substitute.

In his book, *Punishment and Anxiety*, Berg demonstrates this conception of the throttling of the creativity by applying it to sex. He suggests a two-phase genesis of sexual anxiety, passing through similar stages as the monkey did when his expected reward was withheld. Aggression occurs first of all when sexual drives are disturbed. Later a further modification of this aggression leads to frank anxiety. The type of anxiety that stems from throttled creativity nearly always seems to have an element of aggression as a precursor.

Illustrative Case History

At a seminar in which some of the problems of general practice psychiatry were being discussed, a practitioner gave an interesting case history. A patient had consulted him because of a tendon injury to the finger. It had been caused by her suddenly going into her garden and savagely pulling up weeds. The patient was a normal and outwardly calm well-educated woman, who was judged a well-controlled, mature person. She was also a skilled and keen horticulturist. As the doctor splinted her finger he gently asked how she had come to be tending her garden so fiercely that she could rupture one of her finger tendons. The question made her very anxious and she started to sweat. Eventually the following story was volunteered.

The patient had quarrelled with her husband that morning. Apparently they had a disagreement about a long contemplated house move. She wanted to move to a larger house with a bigger garden, but her husband was quite content to stay where they were. They had argued violently, the argument prompting her rush into the garden and to subsequently injure her finger.

The practitioner put forward a Freudian interpretation for this incident. In her rage she wanted to murder her husband, but this, of course, was unthinkable. So in her rage she went out and 'murdered' the weeds instead. A more feasible explanation seems to be that the patient found her garden a satisfactory outlet as far as creativity was concerned. We do not know if her marriage was satisfactory, or if she had a family, or if other channels of creativity were open to her, but evidently the garden was her great joy. Unfortunately it was small, and when the opportunity arrived to obtain a larger one, her husband frustrated her steps in this direction. Her reaction was to become aggressive with her husband and with other things too. The uncovering of her real feelings, in this matter at least, produced the experience of obvious anxiety.

A realization of this sort of cause and effect mechanism as far as anxiety is concerned is, I feel, well worth while, for there seems little doubt that anxiety generated in this way can often be prevented from reaching alarming proportions simply by understanding the mechanisms involved.

Illustrative Case History

A businessman in his mid-fifties originally consulted me because he was worried about his excessive drinking. After one particular drinking bout he had behaved aggressively at home and done considerable damage. This patient, although successful as far as work was concerned had unfortunately married a rather cold and unresponsive woman. His children tended to side with their mother in all important matters and rather looked down upon their father as a 'jumped up little tradesman who'd made good', as he put it.

On examination he showed many of the signs and symptoms of chronic anxiety and admitted that he only felt reasonably happy with himself after he had drunk half a bottle of whisky. He managed to do this on most days. Though this patient had virtually no formal scientific training, like many people of his type he was self-educated to a high degree and had a reasonable insight into his condition.

He quickly accepted that a form of anxiety was making him drink heavily, possibly as a result of a throttling of his life force. His very successful engineering business now practically ran itself. His family were well provided for and made it clear that they had little need of him.

After long discussion he revealed that when he was young he had been trained in a blacksmith's shop and had been very interested in welding in his early business days. It was suggested that these old skills should be relearnt in the large welding department of his present business, when a tangible end product might in some way compensate for the lack of creativity that was affecting his attitude of mind at the moment.

As a result, and with his foreman's help, the patient learned the special techniques involved in using modern high voltage arc welding equipment. Gradually more and more of his spare time was taken up carrying out first of all simple, and later more complicated work of this nature. He felt a great deal better for this outlet for his natural creativity drives and his drinking habits became very much modified.

Perusal of medico-sociological writings provides many similar examples. The way people live and how they spend their spare time frequently affects their state of mind, and is intimately tied up with the genesis of anxiety. Lord Taylor, Vice Chancellor of Memorial University of Newfoundland, said in Montreal recently that it had been proved that a medium-sized town with full employment, good homes, and a varied social life provides the answer to good mental health, and that if such simple provisos are met the overall neurotic potential of the community can be reduced from an average of about 30 per cent right down to 2 or 3 per cent.

Lord Taylor was speaking, of course, from practical experience. The town of Harlow in Essex, which he largely helped to build and mould during the previous eighteen or so years, was a case in point. When he had investigated the neurosis incidence in a euphemous 'new town' some years before he had found a high incidence of nervous anxiety among those citizens who spent a large amount of their leisure time on purely passive entertainment. Hobbies or pastimes, without a reasonable built-in, protective and creative factor, are nearly always useless as far as the prevention of anxiety is concerned.

Work, especially work that one can be proud of, is a psychological stabilizer, and this has been stressed time and time again by those who have appreciated it as a solace from private and personal problems. Two striking examples immediately come to mind from the world of literature.

Illustrative Case History

Thomas Carlyle had a humble upbringing. Son of a Dumfriesshire mason, he was unhappy at school and left Edinburgh University without a degree at the age of twenty-four. His biographers tell us he experienced 'despondency which must have almost amounted to insanity. He was always violently hypochondriacal'. His marriage was of 'dubious felicity' and the moody and unamiable man dragged out a miserable existence in Edinburgh and London in the 1830s.

Although he was adept at writing for the popular press of his age, he found little comfort in contributing to the 'mud, sand and dust magazines', as he called them. He sensed the value of work of a more permanent nature, and hankered after involving himself in a *magnum opus*. Eventually he started to write his epic work on the French Revolution. So great was the relief from feelings of nervous tension and anxiety that accrued from the production of this work that he survived what must be the nightmare of every author – his finished manuscript was burnt under mysterious circumstances while on loan to a friend – and he eagerly set to work rewriting it from scratch – a labour that cost him a further two years.

The success of this work obviously helped Carlyle immensely

with his problems of living, although all his life he remained a difficult and irascible person. His aphorism, 'Blessed is he who has found his work. Let him ask no other blessedness', would seem to deserve a wider appreciation than it has been accorded in our present-day world.

It seems a far cry from the 'bleak, rustic spirit' of Carlyle, 'moaning, shrieking, roaring like a wild wind in some northern and inhospitable land', to the enchanting, yet often troubled kindliness of William Blake. And yet there are similarities between them. Strangely, perhaps, they both published works on the French Revolution, they both suffered from incidents of odd behaviour that today would have earned them, probably, a psychiatric diagnosis, and they both found solace and comfort in creative work.

Blake's feelings on some subjects are difficult to understand, and are often woven around with a fine web of mystical allegory and illusion. But on the soul-saving virtue of creative work his thoughts are simple, straightforward and telling:

I will not reason and compare
My business is to create.

Although disabling anxiety is a terribly common symptom in our world today there is a surprising paucity of evidence of educationists, psychologists or doctors doing anything constructive about it. Indeed there often seems to be more interest in finding ways of increasing anxiety, rather than trying to assuage its ravages. Those whose business it is to artificially generate anxiety in their victims have, albeit unconsciously, often delved deeply into basic aetiology of anxiety in their researches.

The term 'brainwashing' is a relatively new one. There are many methods used, and those whose unpleasant duties lie in this sphere all have their own particular favourite inhuman techniques. On the whole, however, evidence from the victims themselves as to what produces mental breakdown is more convincing than psychological theory.

Most brainwashing procedures involve solitary confinement. Strangely, however, this deprivation of human contact does not seem to produce a great deal of anxiety, possibly because the victim knows it will not be fatal. However uncongenial, cruel or repulsive the prison guards are, an odd type of relationship develops between the prisoner and his mentors which seems to act as a prophylactic against the profound physical loneliness which will affect the state of mind.

Far more conducive to the generation of intolerable anxiety, and the subsequent personality deterioration desired by the brainwasher, is the inactivity of prison life and the continued throttling of creativity. As a result the brainwashed person gradually grows to live in an anxious trance. In this state of induced neuroticism he becomes very easily influenced by any material his captors use in his indoctrination.

A less dramatic example of the genesis of sudden and apparently inexplicable anxiety is seen not among prisoners but in ordinary everyday citizens. I like to think of it as the 'easy street' syndrome. A sudden and perhaps unexpected turn of luck puts someone in a position of instant security. This occurs perhaps in those who have won a large sum on the football pools, or maybe received an unexpected inheritance. After taking a prolonged holiday and surrounding themselves with every possible form of material possession they find that a vague *malaise* overtakes them. Often within months of their good fortune they are glad to go back to quite humble jobs. Creativity denied has broken the back of their new-found security, due to anxiety.

Illustrative Case History

A man of fifty-two had over the previous twenty years built up a promising electronics and electrical engineering business. Through hard work and personal involvement with the development of new processes he eventually became so successful that he was approached by a large international company, and made a very profitable arrangement with them. His firm was at length taken over, and he with them. Nevertheless he retained an executive position on the new board of directors and held a contract for lifetime employment in that capacity.

Almost as soon as the deal was signed he became extremely anxious, his illness taking the form of panic attacks of a very disabling nature. It was suggested to him that his anxiety stemmed from the source we have been discussing in this chapter, and it was explained fully that many folk experience anxiety in this way. Unfortunately there was no response to this form of simple psychotherapy, and depressive symptoms complicated the picture. The patient was referred to a psychiatrist.

Despite everything that modern treatment had to offer he responded only very slowly, and it was not until many months later that the patient felt well enough to pick up the threads of his life again. Needless to say it was very difficult to explain to his wife, a simple person who tended to see everything very much in terms of black and white, why her husband had become ill 'just at the crowning moment of his ambitions'. She could not understand how the sudden blocking of his life's energies could have such a profound effect on his psychological wellbeing. But this was probably the basic cause of his trouble.

A lesser reaction of this sort frequently follows retirement, when men suddenly down tools and stifle the creativity of a lifetime's work. I have argued elsewhere and at some length about the various ways in which the particular hazard of everyday life can be mitigated.[1] The complicated and often obtuse credos of philosophical theologians and the writings and thoughts of the psychiatrist can meet with a degree of unity when the aetiology of anxiety is considered. Paul Tillich summarizes the philosophical point of view by stating that creative processes are available as a protective force in the constant battle the individual wages, to a greater or lesser extent, against anxiety. 'It is not the tools and gadgets that

[1] *Live Long, Stay Young*, Allen & Unwin, London.

are the *telos*, the inner aim of production: it is the production itself. The means are more than means, they are felt as creations, the creative process is felt as divine.'

Gently planting the seeds of a creative act in the mind of someone with a damaged personality, carefully tending the seedling when it germinates and then enthusiastically pruning and training the new plant when it gains strength and flourishes, is really the aim of all occupational therapy. It should be constantly remembered that the ultimate aim of occupational therapy is not bigger and better baskets, transistor radios or even dolls' houses, but a return to the business of creative everyday life.

A psychiatrist, Dr Russell Barton, recently showed us the end product of creativity denied – not in prison, nor as a result of brainwashing, but as a result of long-term detainment in a mental hospital. He coined the phrase 'institutional neurosis' to describe a complex syndrome with its own unique symptoms. Patients are observed to dress, stand, walk in a very typical way, and withdraw into a chronically anxious state of mind. This is brought about not as a result of any particular psychological derangement, but simply because of prolonged incarceration in a mental hospital atmosphere where there has been a lack of any real effort to stimulate vital creativity for many years.

Anxiety generated by the denial of creativity is so common that mankind has, naturally enough, explored various ways of obtaining relief. As stated previously, aggression may assuage anxiety. Sometimes it is possible to fight inner tensions by identifying oneself with an aggressive but acceptable Group or Figure. In other words anxious people by surrendering their personalities, temporarily at least, to certain groups that are behaving aggressively obtain a peace of mind.

Practical examples of this principle operating can be seen in almost any history book or newspaper. It is significant that at times when a reasonably cultivated society accepted cruel and horrific gladiatorial games, or in ages when executions became entertainment, large numbers of previously agrarian folk had been uprooted from the countryside and by dire necessity had gone to live in towns. As a direct result their load of anxiety became heavier and in many cases their natural creativity was denied. This being so, they tended to escape from the pain of this experience in the way we have described.

At other times in history the Church, in its more militant moods and phases, filled the void by providing diversionary activity for its anxiety-ridden children. But rarely in history has a more striking example of escape from anxiety by means of surrender to aggressive groups, been demonstrated than by the rise of the Third Reich in Germany.

In his book *Fear of Freedom* Erich Fromm poses many interesting questions. For instance, does modern man really want freedom or is he afraid of it? Is freedom only the absence of external pressure, or is it the presence of something in itself? Why is freedom for some people a cherished goal and for others a threat? These problems are all socially and psychologically fascinating, and the author relates many of them to the psychology behind the totalitarian regime of the Third Reich. But in his analysis he also draws attention to the relationship between the genesis of mass neurosis and anxiety, and the way society attempts to deal with its painful symptoms. Here is a condensation of his argument.

After the 1918 war, Germany was a place of fallen values. The monarchy towards which the middle class had looked, traditionally and with confidence, for as long as it could remember, was under stress. The Kaiser was being publicly ridiculed and his officers were under attack. Inflation in 1915 wiped out most of the people's savings and any family fortunes that survived this onslaught perished in the Depression after 1929. Within a decade two terrible new facts had to be faced by the German masses: first, thrift was no longer a virtue and secondly, the state could no longer be expected to honour her promises.

When this state of affairs operates there is always a decline in other values. Children who see their parents railing against authority tend naturally to rail against their immediate peers, and the young characteristically look around actively for new leaders – that is, new and worthy sources of authority and therefore comfort.

This situation in Germany led to a large number of people feeling helpless, ineffective and anxious. Some of their anxiety came from a reasonable enough 'alerting' source. For instance, more than a few could not be sure where the next meal was coming from, or how far further down the social scale they were going to slide before things started to improve. But much of the mass anxiety was of a neurotic nature. It probably sprang from many of the sources we have been considering in this book, and not least from the frustration and bottling up of natural creativity.

Work was scarce and unemployment high. The aggressive totalitarian approach of the Nazis rapidly became attractive in the wilderness in which these people floundered. The brutality shown to minority groups allowed them to act out their own helpless, anxious feelings and overcome some of their inability to wrestle with their own personal disasters.

Of course, aggression in the presence of deep-seated anxiety, and experienced by whole peoples as well as individuals, is not limited to events in Nazi Germany.

Fromm's book was published over twenty years ago. It would now be interesting to be able to read his account of the national anxiety in the US, and the symptoms it has produced which are the result of new legislation and shift of governmental opinion with reference to racial integration. Similarly, much that is violent in Rhodesia today springs from the anxiety of the white settler who suddenly sees his hard-won position in jeopardy.

One of the most puzzling things to most people in these islands has been the antisocial and often violent actions of British youth during the post-war years. At a time when social security exists, and a highly comprehensive social service brings full employment, basic anxiety among the young remains high, and symptoms of violence, often of a particularly senseless variety, seem to erupt repeatedly. Conflicts similar to the Mods and Rockers outrage are still reported frequently in the newspapers, and it seems possible that these are caused by anxiety which has at least some of its roots in frustrated creativity.

The trend in industry today is towards mergers. These involve vast sums of money, and always move towards a higher degree of specialization as far as work is concerned. Eventually work for the individual becomes a completely impersonal thing, and he spends his working hours at limited and narrow tasks which apparently have no tangible end product.

Females seem capable of working under these conditions very much more happily than do men, who subconsciously, anyway, feel their life's energy thwarted, and their basic creativity denied by such industrial circumstance.

The way in which such unfortunate folk try to relieve their feelings of anxiety takes many forms. A few withdraw to the seductive half-life of alcoholism or drug-taking. Others struggle above their present lot and move into a world where rewards are more tangible, and life therefore becomes more worth while. Creative, productive and artistic hobbies can fill the void in the lives of others. But there seems to be, at present, an ever increasing minority who find a satisfactory release from intolerably anxious feelings by following the natural, biologic path to fight reactions or to violence. Either by identifying themselves with violent characters, or by association with the uncontrolled aggressive behaviour of others, they find temporary release from anxious pain.

CHAPTER FIVE

The Fear of Reality

In our brief examination of anxiety we have seen several threads of fear, or modified and altered fear, permeating the substance of anxiety. First of all the two false subconscious suppositions were examined, one of which acted because of a sense of deprivation, and another that was preoccupied with the apparently inexplicable nature of things. In the last chapter the disruption of peace of mind due to a blocking of creativity was touched upon, and now finally we must examine something which completes the picture of anxiety–a basic fear of reality.

To start with this may appear to be something of a paradox, for fear by definition may be expected to be either dissolved by cowardice or routed by courage. But this particular type of fear, fear of the real world around us, the world which is unthreatening to the majority, is a very different psychological situation. It is not generated as the result of events that may overwhelm us, or which may be a danger to actual life. It is a fear of the mechanics of life itself. In other words, it may be considered as a special form of anxiety born of a real world which is patently not a source of worry to everyone.

For this situation to be logical and acceptable we must make one rather important assumption. Those who experience this fear of reality must be different, perhaps only in some very slight way, or at rather special times, from the mass of people –for whom the reality of everyday existence is accepted, if not always happily, then at least philosophically. The nature of this difference can be very complex or very simple. Perhaps the most simple of all is a straightforward lack of personality maturation.

In the same way as a puppy will stop and bark at a piece of paper blowing across a street, various real-life and utterly banal situations can make the immature person disturbed and anxious. The differences between the average non-anxious individual and his anxiety-prone brothers and sisters may stem from various conflicts over life which he has not been able to resolve satisfactorily, or maybe have their origins, if we are to believe classical psychiatric dogma, in childhood or even babyhood.

Personally I do not think it is necessary to attempt to explore the inner reaches of the personality too deeply or theoretically to repair some of the anguish caused by a basic fear of reality. First of all it is necessary to examine in a little detail situations that we see around us in everyday life which provoke this fear. One way to do this is to look at the escape mechanisms that mankind has evolved to try to combat painful anxiety generated largely by a fear of reality.

Alcohol might well be looked upon as a specific drug, tailor-made to ameliorate distressing symptoms of this particular form of anxiety. One cannot see it helping very much, except in anaesthetic quantities, in the other types of anxiety we have been discussing, but as far as reality fears are concerned it is, superficially at least, effective and efficient.

Alcohol is a selective and progressive depressant of the central nervous function. When taken in smallish doses it removes, temporarily but surely, the highest and most critical biological functions of the brain. Larger quantities of the drug gradually inhibit the whole of the central nervous system until eventually a state of anaesthetic intoxication is reached.

The anxious and nervous 'social drinker' endeavours to limit his consumption to the phase one state of affairs. Alcohol effectively dampens all the psychic phenomena which are responsible for his anxious reality fears, and he is transported, for a while anyway, into the easy world of his more fortunate fellow creatures. Sometimes this drug-induced confidence is of considerable value. One of the ways in which we all learn to mature is by passing over various achievement hurdles. If confidence follows an excursion into the fearful world of reality as a result of a single drug, it may happen that real, not drug-induced, confidence is given a chance to develop. In this way the personality may well make a valuable step forward along the path of maturation.

Unfortunately with alcohol this does not seem to be a common occurrence. Indeed it is hard to make a convincing case for a 'cure' for this sort of anxiety and lay it at the altar of any tranquillizing drug. To my knowledge no one has satisfactorily explained the dynamics of alcoholism, but there seems no doubt that many people progress from social (anxious) drinking to frank alcoholism, in which life without the drug becomes intolerable and work impossible.

John Dent *(Anxiety and its Treatment)* defines the potential alcoholic as someone who drinks to lessen intolerable anxiety discomforts, and contrasts him with the occasional drinker who uses the drug to increase the pleasure of living. But it is difficult to see how pleasure needs to be purchased in this way, if reality is reasonably unfrightening and rewarding. Nearer to the mark would seem to be the suggestion that alcohol, because of its sedative action, reduces the load of anxiety that has to be borne, if only for a short time, and the addict is pleased to buy this seductive release from his inner tensions, even at some risk to himself.

Erich Fromm *(The Sane Society)* draws a useful comparison between the frequency of suicide and the proportion of alcoholics in various communities, and there seems little doubt that the two are closely related. Some psychiatrists believe that alcoholism is a half-way house between an innate death wish and the natural tendency towards self-preservation. It seems likely that when fears of the real world are very incapacitating, the individual will clutch at solutions that seem to promise salvation, and a handy and easily obtainable one will always be alcohol.

But the fears of real situations that alcohol can allay are usually overcome spontaneously if the individual is given time to learn to cope a little better with his environment. Quite often today we expect a young adult, not so very long out of adolescence, to behave with maturity much too soon after finishing his formal education. Making one's mark in the world is for most people a fairly traumatic experience, and if the young adult is not over-pressed or harried into mature life patterns he will gradually find he does not need recourse to alcoholic or other tranquillizing indulgence.

An association between two of the most prevalent addictions in Western society, alcoholism and gambling, has only recently been appreciated, and the establishment of a gamblers' refuge organization, Gamblers Anonymous, followed closely on the heels of the better-known Alcoholics Anonymous. The reasons that an individual turns towards gambling, which often leads to social degradation, crime, and can even lead to death by suicide, when the inveterate gambler suddenly has to face the fact that he has lost everything, are extremely difficult for non-gamblers to understand.

The drinker, especially in the early stages of his habit, obviously gets some pleasure from his addiction. In fact the memory of the pleasurable but basically unreal world of friends and cronies in which the otherwise anxious hours are whiled away in a semi-alcoholic haze, the times when good fellowship and sociability outweigh the disability of the painful hangover, are the reasons why most alcoholics cannot face the only real cure for their illness, which is undoubtedly a lifelong abstinence from alcohol.

But the whole background of the addictive gambler is socially unattractive and sordid. Bookmakers' premises are seldom, if ever, pleasant meeting places. Occasionally the amenities offered by high-class gambling establishments are pleasant enough, but the gambler rarely makes these part of his interest. In fact, the people who cluster round the tables in both elegant and ordinary gaming houses have a common air of despondency. Watching a group of players as they lose several hundred pounds at the turn of a card or the spin of a wheel, it is difficult to believe that they are having an enjoyable experience. How, therefore, can we explain the fascination of gambling?

A possible explanation is that gambling provides a method of escape from anxiety, an escape organized with some sophistication and one which removes the individual temporarily from unbearable concern about real life problems. Although the actual escape mechanism is not fully understood, the gambler makes a likely psychic package deal which says this: 'Reality and all it implies is too productive of anxiety to be tolerated, for it makes me feel I am solely responsible for everything that happens to me.' The essence of gambling is, of course, a continued flirtation with lady luck. *She* therefore becomes responsible for the gambler's plight, his failures and successes. Nobody can really pass judgement on a man or woman who is out of luck, whether at cards, dice, horses, or even the football pools. And so a measure of peace is 'bought' by excusing oneself of personal responsibility.

Unfortunately, gambling is rarely successful. Although sometimes an individual has a long run of luck that beats, temporarily at least, the laws of chance, the latter are always weighed against the gambler. The gaming saloon must earn a profit, or close. Many severe addicts do, in effect, seem to persevere quite relentlessly throughout a winning phase until bad luck inevitably overtakes them again. Then they feel they have a justifiable excuse to escape from real situations, and withdraw to a world of the 'hard-done-by' and rejected.

But perhaps the most frightening aspect of anxious flight from the real world in present-day society is the flight into drug dependence. In many ways there is a similarity between alcoholic flight from reality and drug addiction, except that in the case of the latter, personality deterioration is more acute, and hopes of remedial therapy rather less likely. The drug addict places himself in most cases, by the illegality of his action, in a position which from the very start is a point or two removed – further even than the alcoholic – from the real world of ordinary people and happenings.

At the present time there is a tendency to discuss drug addiction under two main headings: addiction to soft drugs and addiction to hard drugs. As far as soft drugs are concerned there is a continued movement to place the most popular of these, marihuana, in an intermediate position between the socially accepted addictions, like alcohol and tobacco smoking, and the so-called hard drugs, by which we mean mainly heroin and cocaine. Pressures have been brought to bear, either to legalize marihuana smoking, or at the very least to reduce and limit penalties for being in possession of this drug.

A quite convincing case can be made that long-term addiction to marihuana may well be less damaging to the health than heavy use of alcohol or tobacco, but I think a word of caution to potential or actual 'pot' addicts is not out of place.

Although the long-term effects of marihuana are not well documented from the point of view of pharmacology and pathology, the most common short-term effect of the drug is a sense of dreamy well-being. Habitual use leads to a decline of personal ambition, a loss of sexual desire, a turning away from previously valued social ties, such as family life, and a loss of pride in one's personal appearance. In other words the addict once again makes a psychic package deal with his personality, and accepts willingly the effect the drug has upon him in return for his escape from personal anxiety about the real world.

The use of hallucinogenic drugs is a step in the same direction. It is worthwhile remembering that primitive mankind has used hallucinogens of various types throughout the ages as a psychic mechanism by which intolerable, painful or unattractive reality conditions may be made acceptable, or are avoided. In many cases the use of these is controlled by a specialized member of the community who may be a priest, or hold a quasi-medical position in society. When this state of affairs obtains there is, generally, a periodic withdrawal from reality that often occurs at certain specially prescribed times of the year, and when the whole tribe or community indulges in hallucinogens as part of a strictly controlled ritual.

Because of the antiquity of such practices the modern user, or would-be user, of hallucinogenic drugs has often been able to argue quite strongly in favour of their more general acceptance today. Unfortunately it has been proved without doubt that the reactions to drugs like LSD are by no means predictable – much less so than, for instance, alcohol or other tranquillizing drugs. Even the addicts who lobby for a more permissive attitude to the use of hallucinogens agree that it is possible to have a 'bad trip' after taking them. Then the unreality purchased at the price of the drug experience is occasionally more worrying and anxiety-producing than the everyday world.

Recent work also indicates that the use of the commonly used hallucinogenic drugs does on occasion lead to the development of frank psychosis in someone who otherwise might well be able to cope with life in a reasonably normal way. And so, as aids to escaping from anxiety produced by fears of real-life situations, these drugs must be roundly condemned.

Illustrative Case History

A young post-office worker had a poor employment record due to frequent attacks of fairly severe anxiety. He had been seen by a psychiatrist and was being treated by various tranquillizing drugs and by means of analytical group therapy at a day hospital.

During one of the therapy sessions he became friendly with an ex-university student who had been unable to continue his studies for psychiatric reasons. Unknown to the therapist this patient had fairly wide experience of hallucinogenic drugs, including LSD, and introduced the young postman to this drug. One day a few weeks later the author was called to see this patient because he refused to get out of bed and would not talk to either of his parents. He was very withdrawn and difficult to communicate with, but eventually confessed to being controlled by means of cosmic rays emanating from a satellite. He also believed that as a result of his experiences under LSD he had a new insight into the inner workings of the post office, and that it would be possible to communicate with people by thought letters, thus obviating the necessity for a postal service at all.

Eventually he was seen by a psychiatrist, and the diagnosis of schizophrenia was confirmed. He has remained in hospital in a very disturbed condition.

By far the most common way in which the person for whom life is a frightening and anxiety-ridden experience escapes is by means of simple mechanisms that have nothing to do with any of the common social or other addictions. Every medical student, from his early clinical training, is taught how to differentiate between the symptoms of physical illness and those which are graced with the all-embracing term 'psychosomatic'.

Physical symptoms, of course, stem from a demonstrable pathology, a change in structure of an organ or tissue. The palpitation or rapid beating of the heart, following the mechanical failure of this organ as a pump, may be due to several organic diseases in which altered structure of the heart valves or muscle have occurred. But probably the commonest form of palpitation is due to anxiety, and in this case the symptom is labelled a psychosomatic one.

Now psychosomatic symptoms are often unpleasant. Apart from palpitation they commonly include fainting, shortness of breath, diarrhoea, paralysis or even blindness. Sometimes they are so devastating that it is difficult for lay people to understand what is gained by those who suffer them. Exactly what is *gained* is, however, quite clear. And something of the terrifying experience of severe anxiety may be appreciated by a consideration of these escape channels.

At times the psychosomatic escape from a reality fear is incredibly snugly tailor-made to meet the situation. The actress or pianist who is prevented from doing something with a heavy anxiety tag attached to it, loses her voice, or cannot move her fingers. A student may be so anxious about the result of his examination that biliousness or diarrhoea prevent him from attending the venue of the reality fear, i.e. the examination hall. A mother who finds child-rearing difficult and full of anxiety may become very unsteady on her feet, and complain of giddiness to such a disabling degree that she cannot be expected to cope safely with the little one.

Illustrative Case History

A lady doctor of forty became pregnant aften ten years of marriage. She had been intensively investigated during the previous four years, and although no organic cause could be found for her apparent sterility she was advised to adopt a baby. She opted for a child of two years, and within a few weeks of adopting this toddler she found herself pregnant. She had an uneventful confinement, and apart from being unable to breast-feed looked after her baby perfectly well in hospital. As soon as she arrived home she experienced overwhelming anxiety and foreboding. Although her mother was there to help, and there was adequate social support in the form of a health visitor in regular attendance, she was convinced that she could not cope with life at all.

Her presenting symptom was breathlessness and on examination she appeared to be overbreathing shallowly and rapidly. There was a slight wheeziness of the chest and she had a repetitive nervous cough. X-ray examination showed no abnormality, and it took a considerable amount of reassurance to convince her that she was not a profoundly sick woman. After about a month's intensive treatment for her anxiety and a detailed exploration of its aetiology she gradually became more settled and could look after her baby.

An understanding of the nature of psychosomatic illness and its relationship to anxiety is useful, if it leads to an understanding by friends and relatives of those stricken with these miseries. Clearly nothing can be gained by branding such people as 'inadequate', or even 'lead-swingers', or 'scrimshankers'. The only way they are likely to overcome their disabilities is by the gradual emergence of real confidence in themselves as people.

The psychosomatic symptoms that disable such folk must be accepted for what they are: painful ways of deflecting an even *more* painful anxiety. It may seem a far cry from the case of a middle-aged lady doctor who could not look after her baby, to a young business executive who found, on marriage, that sexual intercourse was completely unrewarding, and whose wife felt he was probably paying attention to another lady. These two cases, however, have quite convincing similarities.

Illustrative Case History

A patient sought advice because his wife was making his life extremely unpleasant for him. She was pitching a series of matrimonial battles whose real cause was the fact that although they had been married only eighteen months or so, he sought sexual contact with her very rarely, perhaps once every month or six weeks.

To start with the patient denied any sexual difficulty, and suggested that it was his wife who was at fault, and that she made excessive sexual demands upon him. When it was pointed out that this was hardly realistic he eventually admitted this and explained that sexual intercourse was, in any case, quite unsatisfactory to him, and he did not see why he should force himself in this way just to please his wife.

On closer questioning about his sexual experience, it was

learned that there had been no premarital sex between the couple and the husband had, in fact, never experienced sexual intercourse with any other woman. He had, however, enjoyed a great sexual satisfaction from mutual masturbation with several girl friends, including his wife, before they were married. He still masturbated frequently to ease sexual tensions. This he judged to be much more satisfactory than coitus.

This type of behaviour is very common in both sexes. Karl Merringer writes (*Love Against Hate*, Harcourt Bros & Co, 1942) that 'the adolescent usually resolves the sexual tensions of puberty first by masturbation, and then by experimental heterosexual relationships of a more or less romantic nature. Finally he rejects these as he begins to be capable of a consistent, stable, constructive and realistic interest in the company of the opposite sex, which indicates his emotional faculties have matured enough for him to make permanent relationships and contemplate marriage'.

Patients of the type referred to in the illustrative case have usually suffered an inhibition of sex maturation, due to a childhood or adolescent experience – perhaps for instance expressions of real masculinity were forbidden or associated with feelings of guilt. This may occur when a powerful mother fixation has been present, or because of a strong, overbearing and masculine father. When this sort of thing occurs, assuming the rôle of the adult male becomes overladen with anxiety; first of all in case he makes mistakes and therefore may be ridiculed, or secondly because he fears he may lose face with his peers in some way. A situation like this tends to lead to the adult male rôle being abandoned (through reality fears). Thus his adult position never develops and he remains permanently 'stuck' in the adolescent plane from the sexual point of view, where sexual fantasy remains attractive and actual physical coitus is unrewarding.

Men who arrive at this position often find themselves playing the part of the philanderer for the rest of their lives. They cannot gain enough insight into their state of mind to understand themselves, and face up to their subconscious fears of real situations with women.

The tragedy of impotence and frigidity, which quite often ruins otherwise happy lives, is all too often due to anxiety in various forms.

Illustrative Case History

A woman of thirty, who was married and had two children, sought advice because of her self-confessed frigidity. She maintained that although she loved her husband, sexual intercourse never interested her. Her sexual coldness had driven her husband to various irregular sex liaisons. Rather than provoke endless argument she had, for many years, condoned his behaviour. Recently however she was becoming worried about her spouse's heavy drinking. Apparently the friend he associated with in his sexual pursuits had a bad influence on him in other ways as well, and was getting him into debt. At a confrontation the husband agreed to give up his extra-marital sexual activities if she would give the marriage a fresh start. Although she very much wanted to do this, her inherent frigidity put her into a terrible position.

The past history of this woman, as it emerged, was extremely interesting. Brought up by rich and rather authoritarian parents, she had been caught when quite young playing at some quite innocent sex game with a small boy cousin. The housekeeper who discovered this childhood episode of simple exploratory sex reported the whole thing to the father, who had reacted violently and quite unreasonably. For years afterwards she had felt herself 'watched over' very carefully by her parents, and was not allowed to go out with friends of the opposite sex at all until she had left school.

She expressed the thought that her parents obviously believed she was a 'sex maniac' of some sort, for they lost no opportunity of discussing, in her presence, any incident that was locally known or was to be found in the newspapers, which demonstrated the 'terrors of sex', and the unworthiness of all sexual experience.

During all this time she admitted to being fascinated with everything that had sexual overtones. She borrowed such erotic literature from school friends as was obtainable, and derived intense satisfaction from the casual sexual interest shown to her by boy friends. All this time, however, she was strongly aware that sex was an absolutely taboo, forbidden subject, at any rate before marriage.

When she met her husband, who was considered very suitable by her parents, the courtship was a whirlwind one and they were married without there being anything very much in the way of sexual knowledge between them. Then, to use her own words, 'sex suddenly died' for her. When her husband made love to her she suffered extreme palpitation and 'thought she would expire'. She never reached orgasm and found the whole experience revolting and curiously frustrating. When asked what palpitation meant, she defined it as 'the sort of heart action that occurs shortly before death'. (She had, in fact, had an aunt who suffered from cardiac failure when she was a child, and this woman often took her hand and placed it on her chest to 'feel how bad' her heart was.)

This case proved very difficult to treat and reference to psychiatric colleagues was singularly unhelpful. Very slowly, however, she improved, after accepting that her symptoms were those of anxiety, produced in her mind by a conditioning process during her childhood and adolescence.

It was explained that a dominating belief had been implanted in her mind during her young days that could be summed up by the phrase, 'sex is forbidden'. As she grew up, however, she was naturally drawn by curiosity to this forbidden subject. Eventually she made a bargain with herself. Her natural sexual drives, which were strong, were in fact forbidden drives and the fascination of them, as a young, developing woman, sprang from their forbidden quality. On marriage she discovered that sex was, patently, not forbidden. The reality of a normal sexual relationship became very unattractive to her, and this made her very anxious.

Her anxiety symptoms were really produced by the unnerving position in which she eventually found herself – that was, married to a man for whom she had no sexual feeling or inclination. Subconsciously, then, she protected herself by a screen of real illness. She knew that someone with a bad heart suffered from palpitations. Naturally therefore, she told herself the palpitations she felt when her husband made love to her might kill her, and therefore coitus could be abandoned legitimately.

By this neurotic logic she convinced herself that she could not be expected to take her rightful place in her marriage. In a nutshell, fear of her real situation, i.e. she was a married woman who should reasonably be expected to make love to her husband, made her so anxious that it drove her to develop psychosomatic symptoms, in this case palpitation, that could excuse her from playing her proper rôle in life.

An even more dramatic flight from real-life sexual situations into anxiety-ridden, neurotic behaviour can also be seen in the development of homosexuality. The male homosexual in all probability develops his unfortunate trait because of a great, and perhaps unconscious, fear of women. The anxiety produced by a real-life situation, i.e. that as men they are expected to court, marry and have children by a woman, is so great that the homosexual flies from it 'in panic to another continent of sexual experience' (*Counterfeit Sex*, Edmund Bergler, Doll, 1962). Having made this flight of anxious panic the male homosexual elaborates, by means of a psychic hoax, an excuse for his abnormal behaviour

Thus he persuades himself to establish his *difference* flamboyantly by assuming the mannerisms and superficial behaviourisms of the very sex that frightens him so much. Homosexual organizations in many countries have fostered the (false) belief that homosexuals of both sexes are in fact a third sex – a sort of sexual *élite* among the commoners of heterosexual society. If such anxiety-ridden behaviour were not so pathetic, the psychological antics of these emotional cripples might well be amusing.

Another situation generated by anxiety about real situations can conveniently be thought of as psychic masochism and psychic sadism. Psychic masochism is perhaps the most common of these. Dostoyevsky in *The Brothers Karamazov* describes the attitude of such a person as a man 'who had a pressing need to find someone to whom he could surrender as quickly as possible that gift of freedom which he, the unfortunate creature was born with'. In practice, however, the victim is more often a woman.

Illustrative Case History

Almost any practice has in its care a 'chronic attender', the patient who comes to see the doctor not once a week, but sometimes twice a day. The patient in question was a woman who first came under care some fifteen years ago. She had unfortunately led a very tragic early life which had resulted in a great lowering of her standard of living, until she found refuge in a small two-roomed maisonette on a County Council housing estate. She complained of such a variety of symptoms that she soon had a large and bulging envelope of medical reports and letters from various hospitals and specialists. As a result, she came under the influence of a number of medical and paramedical organizations, each of which she in turn 'sucked dry' of sympathy because of her incessant demands for attention. Before embarking on such a large-scale dependence on state-organized institutions, she had exhausted the sympathy and understanding of all her friends and family.

Eventually in her old age she developed an organic illness of an incapacitating and painful nature. She ended her days in an institution clamouring, not for a release from her pain, but for an extra share of everything of a material nature that the institute could offer her in terms of attention, food, comforts and so on. To the very end she was, in fact, seeking somebody, or something to surrender to.

It is perhaps difficult to understand that such behaviour is in fact triggered off by anxiety, unless the point is taken that such a person can only escape from her intolerable anxiety about real-life situations by convincing herself, and of course others, that she is an incapable, childlike creature who constantly needs the support and comfort of stronger brothers and sisters. Such patients do not respond to any of the usual medical or psychological treatments for anxiety.

In the early stages an acceptance by the family that there is nothing physically wrong with the victim, and constant reassurance on this point, often prevents some of the worse *sequelae* occurring. For unless a fairly firm hand is taken with a patient of this type she will certainly destroy the lives of others.

Understandably many daughters or spouses who have to cope with such a situation are sorely tempted to 'off-load' their difficult house companion on to the doctor. By constant contact with other patients in the average doctor's waiting room, a psychic masochist can assume an impressive array of symptoms in a very short time which are liable to convince all medical personnel that complicated investigations are necessary. The inherent helplessness of this type of patient from the outset almost invariably impresses specialists, who are all naturally keen not to miss any serious pathology.

Thus someone whose only disability is anxiety about the realities of life is often subjected to numerous investigations and tests, some of which are of a relatively dangerous nature. A rich patient of this sort is liable to 'punish herself' via the medical and paramedical professions even more severely than those less well off, seeking and obtaining the (needless) services of a great number of specialists, fringe practitioners and even quacks.

The handling of such a person naturally enough presents a

terrible problem. A good working idea from the doctor's point of view is to insist upon 'one hospital only' rule, as far as investigations are concerned. The only success I have ever seen in this direction has been through philosophical and religious channels, for fundamentally the psychic masochist is a person who is only likely to be released from anxiety through spiritual conviction, and not by manipulation of real-life situations.

Psychic sadism is the other side of this curious anxiety-marked coin. A fear of reality lies at the bottom of this condition too and sufferers try to buy themselves a little peace of mind at the expense of others, by petty tyranny and domination. This is usually done by making other people entirely dependent upon the psychic sadist. Ofter he can only comfort his own anxiety by reducing others to mere instruments that bend obediently to his will. Such behaviour is, of course, extremely neurotic and abnormal and those who tyrannize in this way frequently provide plots and stories for novelists and writers. Seldom however, has the anxiety-prone nature of the family tyrant been understood by his many chroniclers. It is to true life that we must turn if we wish to see basic fears of reality translated into petty tyranny.

Illustrative Case History

A health visitor approached the author over a family problem. Two children of school age were obviously very emotionally disturbed. A girl of thirteen had started to wet her bed, after having been dry for many years, and a younger boy was getting frequent attacks of asthma that resulted in a lot of time off from school. Their father was manager of a motor-car service station, and had recently been made a director of his firm. Although the family as a whole were under the care of another doctor, the mother was the author's patient.

She appeared a very quiet, down-trodden woman in her early-forties, who came to the consulting rooms only every year or so for one minor ailment or another. At the health visitor's request she specially attended, and an attempt was made to discuss her family problems. To start with she clearly resented this as 'outside interference', but when the motives behind the interview were explained, i.e. the welfare of the children, she broke down and confessed that married life had been a misery for a long time, and had it not been for her religious beliefs she would have sought a divorce.

Her husband was a very 'mean' man about money. He insisted on account books being kept for all domestic expenditure, and these had to be checked by him, with prolonged wrangling, every Sunday night before he would release the next week's housekeeping money. He frequently made inspections around the house rather in the style of a commanding officer, and if he found evidence of dust on a lampshade or over a door architrave he would rant and rave about hygiene and the slovenliness of the household. He also made spot checks on clothes, laundry and a hundred and one other things that are normally a woman's sole responsibility, and missed no opportunity to show her up in front of her relatives, neighbours and children.

On many an occasion, after a particularly humiliating experience, the wife would finally lose her temper and start to make plans to leave her mentor to his own devices. When this happened and it appeared that she really meant it the tyranny suddenly evaporated. Then the husband broke down and often cried, saying how sorry he was, and how much he needed her and the children. He vowed he would mend his ways and in this state of abject misery was forgiven by the wife. Almost within hours of this scene, however, the charade was recommenced, and within days the *status quo* was again maintained.

It was suggested that the next time her husband launched himself on a tyrannical attack it might be a good idea to ask him why he felt so anxious and insecure, but at the same time being quite ready for further 'fireworks' as any confrontation with the real-life situations that were filling him with anxiety would in all probability stimulate him to further aggression.

This in fact occurred. But the wife was encouraged to continue this way of handling her husband's behaviour, and to refuse to allow herself to be treated like a child by him, and to suggest that he looked ill and should see a doctor. Although there was no dramatic change in the situation, gradually things settled down, and the health visitor could report a general improvement in the health of the children.

Doubtless the change in the family situation was brought about more by the wife understanding the mechanics of her husband's behaviour than by any great change in his attitude. When, however, she could understand his curious behaviour she could make it less important in her own eyes and therefore more bearable to herself and her children.

Perhaps the most alarming way in which the individual can behave when faced with painful anxiety brought about by the stress of reality is by destruction of the real situation, which is replaced by a less anxiety-filled reality. This is yet another factor in the development of what happened in the Fascist countries prior to the last war. The dictators and their totalitarian regimes destroyed social systems and countries and even attempted to destroy races in order to create a new and reassuring reality.

A more prevalent withdrawal from reality in this day and age is a withdrawal into a special sort of conformity, a withdrawal into the group. It seems very likely that this instinct is responsible for the popularity enjoyed by many strange types of club and off-beat minority groups. Sometimes this is a harmless defence against anxiety, and it is always worthwhile remembering that fashions change. The present club uniform is rather odd and many of us find it difficult to understand. The hair tends to be worn very long, the clothes are highly coloured and somewhat bizarre and untidy. To the parent generation the aims of the club are rather inexplicable, and the means of achieving them questionable.

Nevertheless, it seems a shame not to make some effort to

understand these youngsters who, by the way they live generally, try to ease reality tensions in a reasonably socially acceptable way. The traditional football field or the tennis court society of older and 'squarer' generations does seem definitely outmoded.

PART II: SPECIAL CASES

We have now examined the main causes of anxiety fairly closely and it is possible to look at some of the special ways in which anxiety presents itself in everyday life. Effective ways of escaping its demoralizing influence can then be explored.

CHAPTER SIX

Anxiety and the Heart

The basic physical response to an anxious situation is, as we have seen, by the bodily reaction of fighting or fleeing. So it is understandable that a heart symptom like palpitation, a rapid beating associated with an abnormal consciousness of the heart beat, tends to be common in anxiety. 'My heart was in my mouth' is a very reasonable way to express a feeling in which the chest seems too small for this suddenly overactive and feverish organ. In long-gone days, before life became sophisticated, the anxiety-primed heart was of course an advantage. Today however the overactive, anxious heart leads to the development of symptoms. Sometimes patients describe these as a 'bumping or thumping – so loud you would think someone else could hear it!'

But this is not the end of the story. Recent evidence suggests that chronic anxiety as such can eventually effect the heart in a permanent physical way too. In other words, physical or somatic symptoms may then be grafted on to psychological ones, as pathological changes occur within the organ.

The effect of an emotional upset on the function of the diseased heart has been known for a very long time. The famous eighteenth-century anatomist and surgeon, John Hunter, suffered in his later years from attacks of the cardiac pain which we call *angina*, and he once remarked to a friend that his life was at the mercy of any fool who annoyed him. In other words, if he became anxious or upset he would experience pain in his chest in exactly the same way as he would do if he over-exerted himself physically. And in this context it is worthwhile remembering that he dropped dead one day just after a particularly acrimonious meeting with the governors of his London hospital.

Exactly how chronic anxiety or worry affects the heart physically is not completely understood. There is little doubt, however, that it acts as a catalyst and encourages other factors that can cause heart trouble. In a large number of people who have had an episode of serious heart disease, i.e. a coronary thrombosis, it has been shown that in nine cases out of ten it was preceded by prolonged, often job-orientated emotional strain, and associated with chronic anxiety.

In many ways the successful individual – foreman, manager or director – selects himself unknowingly for coronary artery disease. The fact that he is successful usually means that he is an intensely competitive and ambitious person. Not only does he meet all necessary business deadlines promptly, but tends to *invent* (neurotic) deadlines for himself as well. It seems likely that in the same way as he winds himself up to meet and conquer each day, he also winds up and tenses up the whole of his circulatory system, which therefore works in a state of increased tone and stress. It has been found that such individuals are seven times more likely to have a heart attack than their more relaxed and easy-going colleagues.

As we have said, exactly how the blood vessels and the heart are damaged by anxiety is not completely understood. Probably chronic stressful anxiety causes a substance known as *epinephrine* to be produced within the body in larger quantities than normal. This stimulates directly that part of the brain concerned in the automatic functions, for instance the control of breathing, the heart rate and so on. There is also a fair amount of evidence which shows that anxiety tends to make the blood rather thicker, and therefore more prone to clotting or thrombosis than is normal. This change can occur even in fit young men, for instance medical students, just prior to taking their examinations. Naturally enough, for a middle-aged man whose arteries already show signs of wear and tear, this tendency can be highly dangerous.

The 'reason' for this curious state of affairs, a quicker than normal clotting time, is once again a very natural one when you come to think for a moment about anxiety as it occurs in nature. Under the stressful situation of, say a fight, an individual may be injured, and if he is wounded he tends to bleed. The people with the thickest, most rapidly clotting blood are the ones least likely to bleed to death, and so once again they survive in larger numbers as a result of natural selection to pass this happy facility on to their offspring.

Everyone would agree that to escape the hazards of cardiac anxiety is highly desirable, and there is a certain amount that can be done on this score. First of all, it is essential to face up to any diagnosed heart disease as fairly and squarely as possible, with the expert aid of an experienced cardiologist, for real situations are, as we have seen, always less anxiety-loaded than frightening suppositions about life and death.

It is also well worthwhile to take every advantage of purely physical measures that improve one's expectation of life. I have gone into this at some length elsewhere (*Live Long, Stay Young*, Allen & Unwin). Gradually, we are beginning to understand why a low body weight, low blood cholesterol and so on, are so much on the credit side as far as the prognosis in heart disease is concerned. Even the anxiety-induced thickening of the blood can be effectively adjusted by means of adequate exercise.

Finally, when one has taken advantage of all these factors, a look over one's psychological shoulder to see how life is being organized from the point of view of built-in anxiety is of the greatest importance. Are we trying to carry an impossible anxiety load because we are in the grip of, perhaps, a supposed deprivation? Has time really caught us by the tail? Are we using the amount of time at our disposal to the greatest effect? Are we, perhaps, terrified in our innermost mind by one of the apparent inexplicables of everyday existence? If this is so, does it mean that subconsciously our spirit is calling out for sustenance? Maybe something very practical can improve our peace of mind, even something as mundane as taking out a larger insurance policy, or stepping up a personal pension fund contribution.

Maybe the anxiety that makes our hearts bound in our chests inexplicably, from time to time, is because our work, with its deadlines, production targets, promotion prospectives and level of profits, has got so removed from the true purpose of living that we are dosing ourselves with a strong and dangerous medicine. Lack of creativity may be dogging us, and it may be that something to handle, polish or fashion with our hands, something which we can feel we have created, is desperately in need at the end of each day.

A patient once remarked, 'My mind is not just in my head, but all over my body', and in many ways this profound and simple thought is particularly apt if we apply it to the heart and the cardiovascular system as a whole. For a disturbance in one part, if it is prolonged, will certainly alter the efficiency of the other.

CHAPTER SEVEN

Anxiety and the Gastro-Intestinal Tract

Anxiety attacks the 'inside', the stomach and the rest of the intestinal tract, in three ways. First of all there is a classical preparation for fight-or-flight, of a most severe and violent type. This reaction is a simple, sudden emptying of the stomach by vomiting, or the bowel due to a massive bowel movement. Obviously, in a really great emergency the fighting and fleeing individual is more effective if his gastro-intestinal tract is empty, and the whole of his circulating blood is therefore capable of being mobilized to provide energy for muscular action.

This extreme type of anxiety reaction is rare in sophisticated situations, but still happens when men are in combat conditions. Several of the more graphically-related war experiences by the post-war American school of writers have included descriptions of this phenomenon. Neither is it unusual for those involved in harrowing road or rail accidents, for instance, to be sick on the spot afterwards.

A slightly modified and more sophisticated variation of this phenomenon is seen when the 'sick-with-fright mechanism' goes off at half-cock. In other words the sphincters, the little circular bands of muscle that separate the stomach from the duodenum, the small bowel from the large bowel and so on, go into spasm. Then there's a feeling of nausea accompanied by excessive flatulence, or an uneasiness of the bowels that may develop into chronic constipation. This type of reaction is common in anxiety conditions in which there is a special sort of fear, a fear of what should not be frightening. In other words, it is the fear of reality we have explored in Chapter Five.

The second main way in which the bowel reacts to anxiety is simply by overactivity. In a way this is a simple enough phenomenon, merely another way of emptying the greater bowl quickly, so that a possible threat can be met with physical efficiency. The whole thing is, however, set up along a more extended time base. The anxiety is more chronic, less constant, but in many ways more dangerous. It has been suggested that this type of internal response is most common when the sufferer is trying desperately to withdraw, or flee if you prefer it, from a potentially anxiety-ridden situation, and yet he knows in his heart of hearts that he must re-engage in the same battle again and again.

When the stomach reacts in this particular way it tends to contract very rapidly and often pushes food out into the next part of the bowel, the duodenum, in a highly acid and poorly digested state. The change is felt as a mild stomach ache and the acid remaining in the poorly digested food in the small intestine gives a feeling of discomfort or soreness. Eventually the food is hurried along, still incompletely digested, into the large bowel, when it tends to ferment and give gas pains.

More severe stress causes the actual lining of the stomach and duodenum to undergo changes in blood supply, which make it very easy for them to get damaged and ulcerated. Tiny ulcers (lack of continuity of surface in a mucous membrane) may form, but these tend to heal quite easily. A persistent irritation, however, erodes the lining of part of the bowel more actively, and eventually the full-blown condition of gastric or duodenal ulceration may appear with all the classical symptoms of a stomach pain that appears either before or just after food. This pain is usually relieved by alkalis, and it is often severe enough to disturb rest at night.

Recently work has been published showing that anxiety

plays a prominent part in the genesis of disease elsewhere than in the upper gastro-intestinal tract. One of the most baffling illnesses of our day and age is ulcerative colitis. Early symptoms of the illness are episodes of diarrhoea in which quantities of blood and mucus are passed. Usually a very small amount of diarrhoea occurs frequently throughout the day and there is also a certain amount of chronic abdominal discomfort or pain. Quite often the patient becomes progressively emaciated as a result of continued looseness of the bowels and repeated blood loss.

The basic facts about ulcerative colitis are well chronicled. It is a disease of young people and far more than half of the cases occur before the patient is thirty years old. It is particularly prevalent in those who are shy, overconscientious, sensitive or emotionally immature. Now it has been demonstrated that patients who cannot express inner feelings of anger or hostility, those who suppose themselves unjustly deprived and cannot rationalize their fears or 'stick up' for themselves, have a colon that is chronically gouged with blood and which is easily damaged. And so, once again, an overdose of anxiety is shown to be a potential danger to the structure of the body, and something to be avoided whenever possible.

Unfortunately once the disease process of ulcerative colitis is fairly established, treatment either by psychological or other methods is disappointing. In many cases surgical removal of comparatively large segments of bowel is the only hope of cure. It should, however, be possible to prevent an anxiety-prone person developing this unpleasant disease by relieving them in the very early stages of the anxiety involved.

If anxiety produces bowel symptoms then every possibility of escape from disabling physical developments should be explored. First of all self-knowledge is important, and the various chapters on personality traits and clues to the psychological factors involved in the production of anxiety should be studied. Then, particularly because a bottling up of resentment, anger and hostility are undoubtedly most frequently involved as trigger mechanisms, steps should be taken to deal with them.

First of all the sufferer should seek someone with whom to talk over the feelings and fears that are particularly troublesome. The choice of counsellor in this exercise must be someone who can be trusted, but also someone who can 'stand aside' and be disinterested to some extent, as far as intimate details are concerned. Spouses, relatives and personal friends are not good counsel in such cases, as they may well be biased by feelings of personal kindliness, and will avoid any comment that might seem hard or over-blunt. The doctor, priest perhaps, or an older person long retired from life's competitive struggle, and yet someone of wide experience in the business of living may be the best person to talk to.

Only when a permanent modification of one's personal attitude to the whole subject of aggression or hostility becomes possible, will anxiety symptoms evaporate. If, as is frequently the case, a supposed colleague or fellow worker is the object of hostility, the sufferer must try to consider the possibility of this person being someone just as prickly, just as sensitive as himself – someone in fact who probably is not in any way devoted to making him unhappy, apprehensive or anxious. People with 'anxious' stomachs must realize that it is terribly important not to withdraw, not to stand aside and feel unjustly hurt and humiliated at an apparent slight as to their worth or position, as this is a negative attitude to take, and one that can only be damaging to the personality as a whole in the end.

Perseverance in this sort of easing-off of tension eventually leads to a sense of being able to see a bothersome situation almost from the point of view of an outsider. Eventually a private mentor, bully or merely a superior can be accepted as someone who often is right, and can be forgiven sometimes for being wrong – somebody just like oneself, in other words. Once this is realized, the anxiety packed tightly into the situation is suddenly eased.

The final way in which anxiety acts on us in a damaging way through our gastro-intestinal tract is when, if you like, paradoxically, it goads the inside to super-activity, and to super-productivity. But this really warrants a separate chapter.

CHAPTER EIGHT

Overweight and Anxiety

The subject of obesity and slimming, possibly the most discussed health topic of the 1960s, is also the least understood from the purely medical point of view. Until comparatively recently the overweight person has been labelled as being greedy, lazy, or sometimes both. Occasionally a more generous attitude has admitted that the eating of normal quantities of unsuitable and especially fattening carbohydrates causes a fair amount of obesity. But on the whole, those who 'just can't lose weight', have been cavalierly treated by their medical attendants who cannot understand just why particular obese patients remain as they are, despite the prescription of numerous slimming pills and stricter and better diets.

Most slimming pills do, in fact 'work': that is, patients who use them do lose weight for a little while. Then any appetite-suppressing action seems to disappear, and a tolerance evolves which makes the drug ineffective. A great number of slimming pills do seem to have another effect on patients: they get fond of them in the same way as they are fond of food, and feel happier when they are taking them. However, they remain just as fat as they were before. Some people even find that 'slimming' pills of certain types make them more hungry, and gradually it is being understood that the problem of simple (not glandular) obesity is not at all a *simple* subject. This is because psychological troubles are very often the real reason for excessive weight.

When you consider food in its most fundamental sense, as

'manna', a divinely provided, life-giving substance of near magical quality, it is almost impossible to dissociate it from something that is essentially good and life-giving. After all, lack of food for long enough means certain death by starvation, even in our sophisticated twentieth-century environment.

From the very beginning of a child's life, food and comfort have alternated, in what must appear a completely haphazard way, with hunger, discomfort, and perhaps anxiety. Psychologists have often underlined this aspect of babyhood by suggesting that, when hungry, a child feels neglected or deprived. A little later the child probably comes to associate mouth (oral) stimulation with pleasure and comfort. He takes considerable pains to sample his little world and find fresh evidence of these much-sought-after pleasures, and so he repeatedly puts things into his mouth, and in this way attempts to increase his personal happiness.

The fat child, the so-called Billy Bunter, is a rejected type of person. He is always the whining outsider, who is not accepted by any of his companions. They bait him unmercifully. Food feeds the poor fellow's soul – he is making up for deprivations in the way of love and esteem by means of overindulgence in oral comfort.

It has also been realized that parents, and especially mothers, often encourage overeating in their children because they cannot feel the love for them that they believe they should. Overfeeding then becomes a comforting compensation for them, and they are saying, in fact, 'If I cannot give you loving care I can at least give you food' and 'I'll make up for the lack of one with extra of the other.'

The adult person who is overweight and who does nothing at all about it, is in nine cases out of ten, unaware of much anxiety. As we have stated time and time again, anxiety is a painful and unpleasant state of affairs. Through eating, these people are producing a comfortable unconscious blanket to cover this anxiety.

Unfortunately there are great and justifiable pressures of a medical nature which are often applied to the overweight person to encourage him to slim. It has been proved repeatedly that simple obesity is a very dangerous condition as far as the heart is concerned. It plays a part in the more dangerous side of blood-pressure illness, and aggravates all types of arthritis.

The tense and anxious person is liable to feel more tense and more anxious when he or she realizes these things, and yet naturally enough will feel even worse if he reduces his food consumption and jettisons his own potent built-in anti-anxiety factor. This, in a nutshell, is the mechanism that lies behind the misery of the failed slimmer.

What therefore is to be done for people who find themselves in this plight? To start with there is one group, those who are severely disabled by their anxieties, and whose overeating is to all intents and purposes allowing them something to live for, who certainly should not attempt to lose weight by dieting until a substantial improvement has taken place in their state of mind. Such patients may be able to come to terms with some of their inner tensions, and understand the mechanisms that trigger off anxiety for them, by learning about the basic causes of anxiety. But generally speaking they need specialized help on a personal level. If they take 'slimming tablets' they often feel hungrier and actually gain weight for the reasons previously stated.

The less severely emotionally disabled overweight person is usually more able to understand the basic framework of his anxiety pattern, by a careful consideration of the common causes of anxiety in everyday life. If he feels that he may be making false suppositions about apparent deprivations as far as love, position, recognition, worldly wealth and so on are concerned, it is a good idea to think carefully about life in general, and consider if perhaps he is aiming his sights too high.

If we seek perfection or high reward in everything, we are almost certainly doomed to failure. Most people know instinctively of something they do well, for fate is certainly kind to all of us in some way. Above all, it is essential to abandon the 'I'm hurt, I'm rejected', feeling. Everybody has their own niche in the world and can be needed, respected and loved by someone. To generate anxiety, because of a feeling of being deprived from a (falsely) anticipated share of the best things in life, is certain folly.

If it seems as though anxiety is being generated in the large powerhouse we have labelled 'lack of creativity', the solution is very much in the hands of the obese sufferer, and the same applies to those whose fears stem from reality problems. Here the practical prelude to weight loss is a scheduling of personal creations and increased awareness of the needs of others. Once the flame of anxiety has been turned down a little, gentle diet reductions can be started and a low-calorie, high-protein diet gradually eases off the weight.

Doctors who are treating such people effectively find that anything remotely resembling a punitive regime, or a diet enforced by a 'what's going to happen to you if you don't do as I say' attitude, is doomed to utter failure.

The failed dieter is first and foremost a failed liver in some plane of his existence. In the large majority of cases he is fundamentally someone who is carrying a load of anxiety too great to be tolerated without some help. He will never become a slim-liner unless his load of tension is lightened.

CHAPTER NINE

Anxiety and Skin Complaints

Patients often find it incredibly difficult to understand that a severe eczema or dermatitis, for instance, can sometimes have nothing to do with detergents, wearing new clothes or something they have eaten. They just cannot accept that all their itchiness, all their scratching and their unpleasant rash is simply a by-product of anxiety of one sort or another. This possibly explains the bewildering variety of skin preparations available on the average chemist's shelf, and patients still tend to try first one and then the other, until eventually when their basic anxiety is temporarily alleviated the last ointment 'works', and gains incidentally a self-perpetuating reputation.

If we go back a little and think about the way in which basic anxiety affects the skin it will be easier to grasp the intimate relationship between the mind and the body's outer covering.

'It made my flesh creep to listen to him' and 'I was terribly hot under the collar', both express bodily sensations arising in the skin as a result of apprehension and fear. We have also seen people go white with fear, or look as pale as a sheet sometimes. Of course at other times we may 'boil' with rage. Blushing, and the hot flushes so characteristic of the change of life in women are, naturally enough, emotional skin reactions too. 'Sweating it out', an expression that tells us that someone is experiencing quite a nasty pattern of anxiety, and 'the hot seat' is generally understood to be the chair whose present incumbent is being put under a lot of anxious pressure.

The 'hot line' between Washington and the Kremlin really describes the feelings of anxiety that hover around anybody picking up this particular 'red' telephone, and even the expression 'turning on the heat' has etymological connections close to anxiety.

The skin, incidentally the largest organ in the body, and the central nervous system, evolve in the embryo, from the same cells, and the former often mirrors quite accurately the tranquillity or disturbance of the latter.

The actual mechanism of the skin's response to anxiety is brought about by changes in its blood supply, changes in the erectability of the hairs it bears, and alternations in the amount of sweat and grease that it produces. The simplest anxiety reactions are fairly crude, and are really an echo of former brutish days. The hair stands on end to make someone look larger, and so fiercer. The increased sweating makes him more difficult to hold in combat, and the blanching of the skin mobilizes body fluids from the great skin blood reservoirs which in turn facilitate greater muscular effort.

The phenomenon of blushing, or even the flushing of the enraged person or of the hormone-depleted woman, is less easy to understand. But it seems likely that this is due to a sudden collapse of local blood-vessel tone which affects the skin in the same way as a sudden collapse of blood-vessel tone in the internal vessels produces the phenomenon of fainting.

Specific Skin Complaints

Acne Vulgaris: It would be brave indeed to incline too strongly to the view that this unpleasant and disfiguring illness has anything very much to do with anxiety. But we know that it occurs generally in adolescence and ends in the late-teens or in the early-twenties. We know, too, that several drug treatments, like long-term medication with antibiotics, or even ultra-violet light, cure or considerably improve most acne troubles.

And yet there are several quite baffling things about acne. Long ago a wise French physician pronounced that it was cured by marriage alone. Adolescent sufferers agree that it is made very much worse by stress, and in many of the worst cases of acne that doctors see there is a preoccupation with the state of the skin that amounts almost to an obsession.

It has been realized for some time that the acne spots are caused through an increase of the amount of sebum or grease that the skin naturally produces. Sebum production surges in adolescence, and all bad acne sufferers have a rather greasy skin. Now it has been demonstrated that the output of sebum from the grease glands in the skin varies with emotion. The normal rate of sebum secretion in a relaxed person can be altered in two ways. During anger, what might be expected happens. Together with increased sweat an increased flow of sebum occurs. This increased greasiness of the skin is an advantage in combat conditions as we have already stated. But in other states of mind, when the anxiety is of a quieter type, when a patient is frozen with fear, depression or guilt, the secretion of skin grease becomes very much reduced.

It is suggested that when this happens, due to exceptionally low flow rates of sebum, plugging of the ducts leading from the glands to the skin occurs. Now in adolescence, mood swings are commonplace, and anxiety reactions of a quiet, reflective nature alternate quite frequently with aggressive fury. If the duct is blocked, an over-secreting gland merely becomes excessively distended, and it is a well-known fact that a distended organ of any type soon becomes hampered by a poor blood supply. In these circumstances, a sebum-producing gland tends to become unhealthy, devitalized and infected by bacteria.

Patients with acne should therefore always look to their emotions and anxieties as carefully as they look to their skin cleaners and lotions. For it seems extremely likely that worry, anxiety and inner tensions will aggravate, if not actually cause, the ugly skin blemishes that make life so miserable for them.

Skin Troubles associated with Itching: One of the most difficult personal situations is intractable itching, and skin itchiness can be brought about in many ways. Some of these are of a straightforward nature, for example the allergic and itchy lump that follows a mosquito bite, or an infestation with the scabies mite.

Much itching is however of an emotional origin, and again the development of our language reflects this. The married man suffers from the 'seven-year itch' when he finds the frustrations and tensions of his emotional relations becoming more than he can cope with. People often are said to be 'itching to get back to work' after an illness, or 'itching' to go on holiday, and 'itchy feet' has become a synonym for travelling. Sexual itchiness occurs too, and it is perfectly obvious that petting or skin stroking is a form of modified scratching. Who has not, at one moment or another, enjoyed an orgiastic if fleeting period of scratching just before going to bed, or for that matter, on getting up?

But there are more medical itchings as well. One of the most distressing conditions that a doctor has to try to deal with, a parent to manage or a patient to put up with, is infantile eczema. Because its course, its extent and its natural history are so variable, together with the fact that doctors know so little of its basic cause, infantile eczema has gathered to itself a great number of names, all incidentally of considerable length. Fundamentally, however, it boils down to an unpleasant skin complaint in which excoriation, bleeding and weeping of the skin occur due to repeated itching or hard rubbing.

Children who suffer from infantile eczema often suffer from asthma as well. Frequently when their skin is bad their chests are not troublesome. Then eventually the skin improves, but an episode of wheeziness incapacitates them. Many theories have been put forward to try to explain both the eczema and the asthma, and it seems likely that several factors combine to produce these attacks. Anxiety and tension, most people agree, play a prominent part in the basic aetiology.

Both conditions are common when a child finds, or supposes himself to be enmeshed in a conflict which acts as a threat to his security. A most common example of this is when the management of a child is quarrelled over frequently. This situation is occasionally seen when a grandmother either chooses or has to take a substantial part in a child's upbringing. When this occurs she often plays a double rôle, posing sometimes as the child's only true friend and loved one, but alternating her attitude with one in which she quarrels with her daughter or daughter-in-law. The essence of this dispute is 'Why am I having to look after this child? He's yours, not mine.' It is not surprising that such a situation produces anxiety in the small creature, who is totally upset by the inexplicable nature of such adult behaviour.

When eczema or dermatitis crops up in an adult, and external irritants and sensitivity reactions to the skin can be excluded, anxiety is usually a causative factor.

Illustrative Case History

The patient was a middle-aged woman of reasonable intelligence, who worked as a civil servant. For years she had suffered from a recurrent itchy rash of the hands that frequently became bad enough to make her stay off work. On several occasions the rash spread to the rest of her body, and she had to be admitted to hospital for treatment. Although her skin condition over the years collected an impressive number of dermatological opinions, there was never any positive evidence of any allergic factor in her disease. Constitutional illnesses were also excluded. It was known that for years she had suffered an unhappy marriage, and eventually her husband got into trouble with the law and received a prison sentence. During this time her skin gave no trouble, only to relapse on his release. In the end she separated from him and now seems to be permanently cured.

Itchy rashes of a nervous type seem to be particularly prevalent when anxiety is fostered by feelings of deprivation.

Commonly this is a feeling of deprivation centred around what are considered to be the patient's rights in the world.

Illustrative Case History

In one large London hospital, two surgeons irritated one another to a high degree, and could scarcely exchange a civil word. Although to one the situation was never really worrying, his senior colleague found even a chance encounter quite alarming from the psychological point of view, and he frequently broke out into a form of eczematous dermatitis on the spot. This would often prevent him from operating for several weeks. Naturally enough, this gave him a perfectly reasonable 'excuse' for absenting himself from the source of his psychological tensions. Eventually he arranged his day in such a way that never, if possible, were he and his colleague together in the same building at the same time. In all probability the unfortunate senior surgeon saw his charming junior a constant threat to his practice, and a potential but unconscious depriver of his professional position or livelihood. As an intelligent man he obviously found his subsconcious anxieties somewhat ridiculous. Nevertheless, his skin showed how much they were upsetting his peace of mind.

Recurrent neurodermatitis of a very similar type often crops up in families in which the home is shared with a mother or mother-in-law. Then either the husband or the wife find themselves in a situation where they feel deprived of position, either as a home-maker or as the ultimate authority in the family. Although domestic harmony appears to reign, a patient with a chronic itchy rash that is not responding to normal treatments may suddenly find himself cured when an elderly relative either goes into hospital or dies.

Significantly, patients who suffer in this way seldom argue or show open aggression. Instead they tend to bottle up their feelings and turn them into intolerable inner tensions.

Finally, before we leave this brief survey of all that is itchy in life, it is worth looking for a few seconds at a condition usually shrugged off as a form of allergy. Urticaria, or hives, is a very common condition. Everyone knows that some people develop an itchy rash after eating oysters, handling plants, imbibing certain drinks with colour additives in them, being stung by a bee, or even after being exposed to strong sunlight. So it is tempting to assume that all urticaria, or nettlerash, is caused by an allergy. It has recently been pointed out, however, that in at least half the cases of urticaria there is no known physical cause and anxiety is often responsible.

Sometimes urticaria breaks out when a person is under tension of a time-deprivation type – a deadline has to be met, or an examination taken. Girls often suffer from recurrent and sometimes alarming 'giant' urticaria, in which the itchy weals are so large that they meet one with the other, and completely distort the features, when the girl becomes disturbed because of anxious reality fears with sexual overtones.

Illustrative Case History

A young girl was seen as an emergency, because of giant urticaria which became so pronounced that her face was unrecognizable, and her eyes were completely closed. There was nothing in her medical history or recent activity to suggest that an allergic factor was at work. But it was noticed that on one of her very swollen fingers there was a very new and sparkling engagement ring. She was also being hovered over, with the greatest solicitude, by a most ardent and concerned fiancé.

Quite soon after an injection of a potent quick-acting tranquillizer the urticaria started to subside. At a later consultation it was learned that she was very anxious about the sexual side of her forthcoming marriage. She had no sexual attraction towards the young man to whom she was engaged. She saw him as a very nice person who had whisked her off her feet, but when the reality of the situation eventually dawned upon her she became very anxious and worried. She developed indigestion and palpitation and eventually the attack of giant urticaria occurred.

The successful treatment of the so-called psychocutaneous disorders is a very good example of patient-doctor cooperation. Once the diagnosis has been firmly made, the patient must try to understand her condition of mind. At times a change in the way in which an individual lives must be made if she is to be permanently free of her troublesome symptoms. Alternatively, at other times all that is necessary is to allow sufficient time for the patient to grow up and out of her disability, in other words to mature emotionally.

As far as local treatment is concerned, quite clearly the simplest possible preparation that affords effective relief should be used on the skin, and great care taken not to experiment with patent medicaments, for these may add a sensitizing factor to an otherwise simple skin-bound anxiety reaction.

If the doctor decides to treat the underlying anxiety by means of drugs these must be taken over a considerable period, regularly, and strictly in accordance with medical advice. Usually this means taking them even long after the actual skin condition apparently settles down.

CHAPTER TEN

The Special Anxieties of Women

As previously mentioned in Chapter Four, there is no doubt that women are more robust creatures than men. They live longer and have a greater expectation of life at all ages than do men. Although the sexes are equally prone to many diseases, certain illnesses are less severe in women, And yet the paradox is that women consult doctors far more frequently than do men, and various reasons have been put forward to explain this phenomenon.

It has often been suggested that firstly, this is simply because a woman's everyday schedule fits into doctors' consulting hours more conveniently than does that of the average male member of the community, and secondly, they certainly seem more prone to deprivation anxiety. But another reason, surely, is that women have a rather more complex reproductive apparatus than men, and that more than occasionally it gives cause for concern and worry.

For years now psychologists have been trying to explain why women tend to be excessively anxious, and two main theories have evolved. First it has been put forward that women in modern society have moved further from nature than men, and secondly that there is a special female infectability as far as anxiety is concerned.

The suggestion that women experience extra anxiety due to a movement away from their natural way of life can best be seen against a backdrop of deprivation, and denial of creativity. Until a little more than a hundred years ago a woman's life was a very domestic affair, and revolved around the production of children. But apart from the fact that modern families are much smaller, soon begotten and relatively soon reared, the creativity surrounding the act has been eroded today. The education of the children also came within a woman's domestic sphere, but nowadays she is deprived of this aspect of mothering by efficient and universal schooling.

Leaving aside the alteration of woman's rôle as far as child-birth and child-rearing is concerned, modern life has made profound changes in the character of her home life as well. Although the majority of women see the vast changes that have taken place, due to different methods of food production, house cleaning, house decoration, clothing manufacture, cleaning and maintenance as advantages, the fact remains that this 'new deal' has removed something from the creative side of home-making.

The female conscious mind also rejoices at everything the food manufacturer and labour-saving designer has to offer – yet it is possible that her psyche mourns, albeit unconsciously, for the time when she was more of a king-pin from the domestic point of view, and less of a well-uniformed distributor of many manufacturers' products, within her home and family circle.

The other change that may have made today's woman more anxiety-prone relates to the nature of her work outside the family. Almost always she has a period before marriage when she works commercially. Sometimes, of course, she will work all through her married life. Increasingly often she seeks employment after she has reared her small family. Unfortunately, commercial work is generally speaking less rewarding for women than it is for men. To begin with, even if they do the same job they are less well paid. Traditionally, they are often employed on very boring, repetitive work, in which there is little in the way of an 'end product', when the day is over. These are all factors that generate anxiety due to lack of creativity.

In most ways, however, anxiety affects women in exactly the same way it does men, except that it has an extra physiological system within which to demonstrate its physical ravages. Anxiety can stop a woman's periods, even to the extent of making her feel she is pregnant, and indeed she may develop on occasion a pregnancy-like swelling of her abdomen. Anxiety can also make her periods excessive enough for her to become physically ill from anaemia. Anxiety has been known to make labour long and a confinement difficult. If anxiety is concerned with the sexual sphere it can make sexual intercourse difficult and even painful. It can also destroy her normal sexual feelings and produce frigidity. If a woman becomes anxious because she cannot produce a baby, anxiety alone can make her temporarily sterile.

But by far the most disturbing area of anxiety as far as the female is concerned relates to painful periods (dysmenorrhea), and this is where the contagious nature of female anxiety is best demonstrated. It also gives another example of how inexplicable occurrences can spontaneously generate anxiety.

The mother-daughter relationship is, at its best, an intimate one, and when this is the case there is, from the very earliest time, a subconscious feeling that they are both members of a rather exclusive female club. If the mother is a well-integrated and not particularly anxious person she will, naturally enough, be pleased to supervise the enrolment of her child into womanhood with quiet pride, and will prepare her in a sensible way for this important and exciting debut.

Not all women are, however, capable of helping their daughters in this way. Some accept the badge of femininity with resentment. When this occurs it is very likely that the daughter will be profoundly influenced by her mother's attitude. She will tend to regard everything female in the sexual sphere with a somewhat jaundiced eye. Menstruation in particular will then be thought of as a messy, unpleasant and above all painful business. When this happens the periods are referred to as 'the curse' of womanhood.

Doctors frequently see girls complaining of painful periods. In some cases they have been completely unaware that menstruation was to be expected (it therefore comes as an 'inexplicable' occurrence), in other cases the painful nature of the process has been stressed by the mother who herself is often considerably disturbed by her periods.

This must not, of course, be taken to mean that all menstrual pain is of psychological origin and is related to anxiety. In most young girls the periods are quite painless for the first two years. Dysmenorrhea, if it is to become a problem, only does so when a woman becomes fertile and starts releasing egg cells from her ovaries each month.

But just how much anxiety is involved in magnifying this true menstrual pain is demonstrated by a current method of treating severe dysmenorrhea, not with pain killers but with drugs that stop egg cell production in exactly the same way as does the contraceptive pill.

The scheme of treatment is as follows. The girl is allowed, by means of drugs, to have two or three anovular (eggless) periods. Only in quite exceptional circumstances are these in any way painful. Having therefore experienced several painless periods she become much less anxious about the 'curse', and usually reacts well to the suggestion that she might like to stop the pills, and see how she gets on without them. A firm assurance is given at this stage that if she feels she needs help again it will be forthcoming. A surprising number of young women who are treated in this way find they can cope with their painful periods quite adequately, without pain magnified by needless anxiety, in the quiet knowledge that if things get too bad they can ask for help again.

Finally, no chapter on anxiety and women would be complete without reference to a troublesome phenomenon common in more middle-aged women, known as premenstrual tension. Although this condition is usually premenstrual, that is, it is most troublesome just before the period commences, in many ways the title is a misnomer, for some patients experience symptoms all through the last half of the menstrual cycle, and even during menstruation. The symptoms of premenstrual tension are very variable, but most doctors would agree that the triad of symptoms – depression, irritability, lethargy – is always diagnostic.

Many women who experience this trouble also complain of being extremely apprehensive and anxious, and for no obvious reason. Quite often they become extremely difficult to live with during the period of tension, and their families often seek treatment for them. Now although anxiety is a frequent symptom in premenstrual tension it seems likely that this illness has nothing to do with the sort of induced anxiety we have been dealing with in this book. One of the most constant findings in premenstrual tension is that the body retains more fluid within its tissues than is normal. Possibly this fluid retention, as it is called, affects the central nervous system in some way, giving us yet another inkling that at fundamental cellular levels all anxiety is due to subtle changes in body chemistry.

CHAPTER ELEVEN

Explosive Anxiety

Panic can be experienced in two ways. It can occur at a purely personal level, and when this happens the individual feels as though he is disintegrating, or exploding. But also sometimes, panic in the midst of a supposedly inexplicable or inescapable situation results in mass symptoms, when large groups of people suddenly behave illogically, without due regard for the safety of themselves or others. This is the panic of the mob trying to escape a fire in a theatre, or a disaster situation like a flood or earthquake. Anxiety in this context suddenly becomes acutely infectious and spreads like wildfire.

The personal panic attack is a very terrifying experience. The patient often feels he is dying, or is about to die. A low level of anxiety may previously have been present for some time, and may have been coped with quite effectively, suddenly flares up spontaneously and is magnified into terrible proportions. One of the characteristics of panic attacks is that they occur in the large majority of cases only when there is an audience present. This must not be thought of as an unkind criticism, for there is no evidence of a true panic attack being something that is 'put on' by the patient to impress a relative or friend. The physical effects are much too terrifying for that to be at all feasible, but it does seem that there is a need for a second person, who in some way acts as a catalyst.

Attacks of explosive anxiety tend to vary in the way they affect patients. Usually there is a certain amount of overbreathing, panting or gasping for air at these times. The heart beats violently, causing palpitation, and the patient becomes very restless, either turning from side to side if he is in bed or tending to pace the room like a caged lion if he is up and about. That panic attacks can be potentially dangerous physically seems very likely, for patients who have been closely examined during such a period of acute anxiety often have an abnormal electrocardiographic tracing and a very high blood pressure.

The trained observer will also notice other classical features of anxiety. Profuse sweating occurs, the pupils of the eyes are dilated, and on occasions, if over-breathing is unduly prolonged, odd feelings are experienced by the patient in the limbs and fingers. Sometimes the patient complains of painful muscle cramps of the fingers, hands or legs.

Although the relationship between a true panic attack and the flight-or-fight response that we have seen previously in anxiety, is very obvious, the panic attack in many ways deserves special mention because it sometimes heralds the approach of another illness, and one that is rather more dangerous than anxiety alone.

Illustrative Case History

A patient sought a consultation because he had a difference of opinion with his own doctor. Apparently he had called the physician from his bed in the middle of the night because he 'woke up in a terrible state', and felt his end had come. By the time the doctor arrived he had taken a glass of brandy at the suggestion of his wife, but he was still very breathless and apprehensive. After making an examination the doctor diagnosed a 'panic attack', and upbraided him for calling him out of bed for something that would have passed in a short time anyway.

Although this man seemed quite stable mentally when first seen, and made no bones about his opinion of the doctor who had had little sympathy for him when he had felt so ill, within a few weeks his general condition had deteriorated. He experienced repeated attacks of the same nature, and significantly these always occurred just before events that he supposed would be stressful, for example a long flight or a business meeting. Therefore they were assumed to be directly related to some specific anxiety. Eventually, however, it became very obvious that his panic attacks were a prelude to the development of a depressive illness, which in his case proved to be very disabling and slow to respond to treatment.

In all cases where psychological problems seem to be responsible for someone's unusual symptoms or behaviour the opinion of a physician should be sought so that an accurate diagnosis can be made. But where panic attacks occur it is even more necessary to continuously exclude organic diseases. There are a number of purely medical conditions that mimic the anxiety panic-attack reaction, and whenever possible family and friends should try to help the doctor with his diagnosis by filling in the background situation, both physical and emotional. First-hand information received from the patient himself may often be extremely unhelpful in such cases.

Closely allied to the classical panic attack is a particular variety of hysteria. Hysteria is in many ways still a mysterious illness. Thought by the ancients to be an exclusively female disease, produced by the womb moving about in the body, we know now it also occurs quite frequently in men. Although the majority of hysterical manifestations are of a relatively quiet nature, for example hysterical paralysis or loss of an area of skin sensation, a form exists in which there seems to be a concentration of the hysterical impulse on the motor system of the body.

When this happens there is often a lot of over-breathing, and a compulsive throwing about of limbs, and so on. So-called hysterical fits, like panic attacks, occur only in the presence of an audience, and it may be that both these states represent a 'cry for help' in a rather heavily disguised form from an over-anxious and sick person.

There is a certain amount of evidence that both the classical panic attack and the hysterical manifestations we have been describing occasionally have some therapeutic or healing effect on the patient who experiences them. Exactly why this should be so is quite inexplicable in our present state of knowledge, but an analogy can give a superficial insight into what is happening.

A simple electrical experiment from the schoolroom may well be remembered. A high electrical voltage is given to a metal sphere by means of a machine that develops electrostatic charges. When another similar metal sphere, but one which is earthed and which therefore has no electrostatic charge, is brought near to the charged globe, at a certain distance a spark jumps between the two as the electricity overcomes the resistance of the air that separates them.

In both panic attacks and hysteria, in which there are great restlessness and tension, intense motor activity of the body seems in many ways to resemble the transfer of energy that equates the electrical charges in the experiment described.

The psychological equivalent of this strange phenomenon has been used in the treatment of certain disturbed states of mind, and has been graced with the name of abreaction therapy. Actual techniques vary, but broadly speaking the anxious patient is brought into a state of high excitability, either by breathing in small quantities of ether vapour or by the injection of a drug. Then he is 'led' by the therapist into the particular anxiety-producing or worrying situation that appears to be responsible for his symptoms. When this happens the patient often behaves very violently, shouting or screaming as he relives, as it were, under the influence of the drug the particular life situations that disturb him.

At one time it was thought that what was said during abreaction was particularly significant, and psychoanalysts often deduced what was wrong with their patients from detailed study of such 'vocalizations' from the subconscious mind. Nowadays it is more widely believed that the physical activity during abreaction is the important therapeutic tool.

One of the big differences between the psychiatric casualties that occurred during the First World War and those of the Second, was the relatively few cases of 'shell shock' after the latter. Though in the period after 1918, shell shock ruined many lives and reduced countless dependant families to penury, the condition was very seldom seen after 1945, and very possibly this was due to advances in psychiatric treatment and a better management of battle-fatigued casualties.

One of the methods of treating those whose psychological balance was disturbed by profound anxiety in combat was by abreactive techniques. Ether was often used and the procedure was as follows. The patient inhaled ether from an anaesthetist's mask, held a little way from his face. Then he was encouraged to talk about his past experiences. As he became engrossed in his story the mask was held a little closer to his face, so that he became mildly intoxicated and partially anaesthetized. If the patient was going to abreact, and it must be stated that not everyone responds in this way, he tended to become violent. It was found to be important to hold patients at this stage of abreaction, for this intensified the excitement. Gradually a crescendo of panic reactions was reached and violence occurred. This extreme agitation is followed by a period of virtual collapse and limpness. When the patient finally 'comes round', he is observed to be composed and rational. He also experiences a distinct relief from anxiety.

There seems to be a striking similarity between this artificial panic reaction and several observed details of human behaviour. It may appear to be a long way from the psychiatrist's couch to a drunken spree of a party of sailors who suddenly find themselves safely in port after an anxiety-filled and probably tense voyage. But there is no doubt that seafaring men have often obtained a release from tension in this way. Certain religious sects throughout the world have used something akin to abreaction to obtain inner peace of mind for their devoted followers.

Dr William Sargant, a well-known champion of physical

methods in the treatment of psychiatric illness, recently told of his experiences among local healers of mental troubles in Africa, at a meeting of the section of Psychiatry at the Royal Society of Medicine. In Ethiopia, a Coptic priest's technique was to spray jets of (holy) water into the faces of those suffering from a variety of anxiety states in which they believed they were possessed by devils. This is a frightening experience for the patient, who feels he is likely to be drowned during the treatment. Often it leads to frenzied excitement, and is followed by a sudden collapse. After this the patient seems to be cured, and enjoys a great relief from tension.

Elsewhere in Africa various other procedures are used to bring about this 'little death', as the collapse phenomenon is called. Although the author would not go so far as to recommend a return to Voodoo for anxious or panicky people in these islands, physical activity extended to the pitch of being completely 'played out' seems to offer a protective or healing effect on profound psychological tensions.

Mankind has obviously evolved over the years many short cuts to rid himself of intolerable states of anxiety. Sometimes these have been socially unacceptable and deleterious to physical well-being. Perhaps a greater personal participation in exciting and strenuous physical games would be of greater benefit than we realize in our efforts to escape from painful and disabling anxiety in everyday life.

CHAPTER TWELVE

Anxiety in Children

Some of the basic differences between anxiety and fear are shown in particularly sharp relief where babies and young children are concerned. Tiny babies, up to the first year of life, respond to fear by crying, or sometimes by trembling, or by a curious jaw-shuddering movement in which the mouth is partially opened and closed every second or so, the whole episode being repeated for several minutes. Sudden noises frighten tiny babies, and so do unexpected changes in position. They also seem frightened by being held loosely, and perhaps this is why bathing is so often upsetting to them. At around the age of six months a strange voice, or a strange place which gives unusual echoes, is frequently terrifying. All these things are probably sensed by the immature mind of the child to be threats to his security, and are therefore fearful.

Some psychiatrists seem unable to overcome their enthusiasm for chosen ideological theory in the understanding and development of anxiety and neurosis. Therefore they tend to 'mould' valuable first-hand observations to fit into the pattern of what they believe to be the aetiology of childhood anxiety. When this happens rarely do they make a real contribution towards the sensible upbringing of children.

For instance, it has been suggested that the apparently panic-stricken crying of a hungry child is brought about by an inner conviction that its mother is going to starve it, or chop it up and devour it! And that sexual overtones, admittedly set in the widest possible terms, are responsible for much that seems otherwise inexplicable in children's neurotic behaviour. Observation of hundreds of children over the last twenty years or so has convinced me that such theories are completely useless from the practical point of view, and are therefore better forgotten.

Anxiety doubtless occurs even in fairly tiny children, and perhaps the most important thing to remember in all child care is that human babies are very immature creatures who have no sense of time. They also vary widely in their needs for food and comfort. A pretty common illness in the very young, three-month colic, is characterized by prolonged attacks of crying, associated with extreme restlessness and distress. This may well be caused by a baby being born with an immature gastro-intestinal tract, for certainly as he develops more fully he finds it easier to deal with food, and the troublesome tummy pains settle down spontaneously.

But there may be other nervous factors that are responsible too. I do not think there is any doubt that a baby who wakes up hungry, and possibly wet, feels uncomfortable, and may experience feelings of anxiety due to the immaturity of his personality as well as that of his bowels. Somewhere in the back of his mind is the knowledge that his mother can put all this discomfort right quite quickly, and he cries to communicate with her. Unfortunately, this does not always coincide with his feed time, and mother may well be busy doing other things. There is, therefore, some delay in taking him up, and because this interval can seem an eternity to him, his anxious and distressed feelings are magnified. Parents, especially when caring for a first baby, are often afraid of 'spoiling' him by picking him up when he cries. Often this desire to feel 'in command' of a baby is dangerous.

But the largest load of anxiety in children is most probably transmitted to the child by its mother, or by other attendants. Dr H. C. Cameron, a quite outstanding observer of children, drew a comparison between the behaviour of very young children and that of birds under stress. Chicks and fledglings can be handled, photographed or fed without showing any signs of being upset or disturbed, provided the mother bird is far away. If, however, she is nearby her own agitation is communicated to the brood with the utmost rapidity.

The infectious nature of anxiety has been stressed in the previous chapter, and it will be, of course, a very unusual and careful mother who fails to communicate something of her own personal irrational anxieties, for instance fearsome feelings about the dark, thunder, heights, certain animals and so on, to her small children. In this way inexplicable anxiety is transmitted within the family.

Sometimes, indeed, children become anxious because of a subtle difference in a mother's tone of voice. The admonition, 'Don't be frightened of the nice doggy!' is hardly likely to be convincing if the nice doggy in question is barking, jumping about and likely to knock down anybody who happens to be around. And if somewhere buried in the back of the mother's subconscious mind is the knowledge that some day, somewhere, she read about or saw a dog that seriously injured a baby or tiny child.

From the very start of life the only child is undoubtedly at an increased risk as far as anxiety is concerned. The adage that a mother's anxious fears, and a father's pride and joy are often too much for a tiny child to be able to bear, is surely true. All through the only child's early life the anxious, protective hand is liable to be there, and it is natural that adult concern is handed over to him in far larger doses than is normal, together with his rather larger sum of weekly pocket money.

The child of a larger family is in a happier position. At first, of course, his reliance on his mother is absolute, as it is with all children, but then, purely due to domestic competition for the mother's time, the apron strings must be loosened and confidence through experience starts to develop. The anxious, difficult child has usually been excessively mothered during a prolonged nursery stage. Already the moments of excursion into his own world have been strictly limited due to parental anxiety, and so he cannot be blamed for looking to the adults around him, what they say, or even the expressions on their faces, for constant approval and for confidence.

In other words the first steps along the road to freedom from anxiety have been diverted, if not completely stopped. The damage that may occur to such a child's psyche, should a sudden and often unheralded intruder come into the family, is immense, and anxiety then flows over him in all the classical ways. Frequently this youngster tends to try to solve his problems and escape from his painful and anxious feelings of being inexplicably deprived by regressing to long-forgotten and abandoned types of baby behaviour.

A brief examination of some of the common problems of nervousness and anxiety in children, and how they relate to the more general aspects of anxiety, follows.

Thumb or finger sucking

This is an interesting subject because it is both an anxiety escape mechanism in children and a potent cause of anxiety to mothers! First of all it is important to state that thumb-sucking is a harmless condition, provided that it stops by the time a child is six years old. Even if it persists after this, the only damage that may be done is to the shape of the child's teeth, and to the pride of the parents who feel that somehow they have failed in the upbringing of their offspring.

I do not think there is any doubt that although thumb-sucking is so common as to be considered virtually normal, it *is* more frequently seen in children whose mothers were too hasty in extending the time between feeds, or constantly hurried feeding times during babyhood. In fact it has been possible to produce paw-sucking, experimentally, in puppies by tinkering with their feeding routines in a similar way.

Because prolonged thumb-sucking is liable to be an embarrassment to parents and a point of ridicule as far as the older child is concerned, it seems reasonable to try to work out ways of dealing with it. Most successful are remedial measures that are taken as soon as thumb-sucking is first noticed.

The thumb-sucker uses this device to obtain the comfort that in some way he feels he needs. He should therefore be given a more frequent opportunity to feed, at either breast or bottle, and if this does not provide the answer a dummy or comforter should be offered as a substitute for the thumb or finger. The primitive desire to suck is, like all primitive drives, a very variable thing and to a certain extent hereditary tendencies alter matters too. Usually this urge to suck is greatest during the first four months of life, and then tapers off at around seven months. But every baby is different in his individual development, and so may take to sucking his finger or thumb at almost any time.

Many mothers still tend to go by what the book, or what the 'lady at the clinic' says, far too rigidly even today. Although a baby gets the large majority of the food he needs during the first five minutes of feeding, if he wants to continue half-feeding and half-sleeping, even for thirty minutes or three-quarters of an hour, then he should be indulged in this way. This is his way of insulating himself against his own basic feelings of insecurity by completely natural methods.

Thumb-sucking, if it is to occur in a bottle-fed baby, usually starts at the time when he is able to finish his bottle within ten minutes or so. Once again he is completely fed, but not completely comforted by his brief contact with his mother, or whoever else gives him his feed.

When thumb-sucking is an established habit, say in a one year old child, it will probably persist for several years. Some children, of course, suck something other than their thumb or fingers, and perhaps a rag doll or even a piece of material is taken as a substitute. Usually the episodes of sucking are limited to moments when the child feels tired or perhaps bored, and then it is best to try to forget all about it and patiently wait for the habit to be abandoned. If, however, thumb-sucking becomes a major preoccupation with a toddler, parents should carefully think things over to see if there is anything in their family life which produces anxiety for the child.

Anxiety in children often springs from frustration of natural creativity urges – that is, playing and exploring. A child confined too much in a play-pen, high chair or even pram, seems to suffer in this way particularly. If during the relatively short time he is unrestricted he is constantly nagged by a 'Don't do that!' type of mother, the effect is to make him more anxious. Children are also very sensitive, as we have seen, to adult emotions and tensions. Although they have no inkling of what lies behind perhaps an innocent enough family argument, there is no doubt that this sudden and apparently inexplicable change in what is happening generates quite frightening anxiety in some children.

It is folly to put unpleasant-tasting things on his fingers or thumb, or to nag him when he starts to suck them. He uses this simple device because he is tired, bored and anxious, and so any punitive methods are doomed to failure because they only give greater *cause* for thumb-sucking. Occasionally an older child will ask a parent to help him stop sucking his thumb. This often happens when he is being teased about it at school, or by his friends, and here one should encourage a more grown-up attitude in other directions which make him feel more important and responsible than he does at present. Then there is a very good chance of this infantile habit being abandoned.

Close to thumb-sucking from the psychological point of view are head-banging, cot-rocking, odd stroking habits, ear-pulling, hair-twisting, nail-biting and nose-picking. Most of these start rather later in life than sucking habits and run a very variable course. They should all be quietly noted by parents and regarded as possible symptoms of a child's anxiety. Often there are straightforward solutions along the lines suggested for thumb-sucking.

Bed-wetting

The whole background of the medical treatment of bed-wetting is one of the worst examples of the lack of insight of a learned profession into a problem of human relationships; and it seems quite extraordinary that many doctors, and nurses for that matter, find it so terribly difficult to observe and understand the behaviour of their young charges.

During the last twenty-five years some extraordinarily odd treatments have been urged for nocturnal enuresis, or bed-wetting. For instance, the operations of circumcision, removing the tonsils and adenoids, injection of saline solution into the skin of the pubic and perineal area have at various times held sway within the profession. Then there have been advocates of mechanical over-distension of the bladder, putting blocks under the foot of the bed, waking the child artificially at night, either by an alarm clock or by an electric buzzer that sounds automatically if a bed is soaked and a host of other fatuous contrivances.

Drugs like ephedrine that tend to paralyse the bladder temporarily have been used extensively, and so have various systems of punishment and humiliation of greater and less severity. Readers of a recent book about life in a well-known charitable institution that cares for destitute children in Great Britain will remember the most popular treatment given there some years ago, which was to rub the unfortunate boys' and girls' faces into their wet sheets in the morning.

Only quite recently have the dynamics of bed-wetting really been given any scientific and objective analysis. Dr R. C. MacKeith, physician to the children's department at Guy's Hospital in London, lectured delegates to a BMA conference in 1968, on the natural history of bed-wetting. He showed convincingly that the percentage of children who eventually obtain bladder control rose from 0 per cent in the first year of life and reached a peak at about the age of three. Then it fell quite rapidly; until after the age of five it is very low indeed, and once the age of six is past, only about 1 to 2 per cent of children then become dry.

Some genetic variation obviously occurs for all body maturation systems. And so, if we take the age of one and a half to four and a half as outside limits, most children naturally become dry within this age group. The reasons for this NOT happening are obviously the reasons for the child remaining a bed-wetter. Dr MacKeith firmly believes that bed-wetting is primarily due to anxiety occurring around the third year of life, and this period is, of course, a time when anxiety can seriously affect a youngster in other ways besides.

This is the time when, due to the arrival of another baby in the family, a toddler first feels painful separation-anxiety, especially if mother has to go into hospital to have the new baby.

Then again if, for instance, an elder child has been dry at about this time, a younger one, especially if mother is an over-busy creature, may be made to feel he is losing face and becomes anxiously ashamed because he has not a 'nice, dry bed in the morning, as his big brother had at his age'.

Sometimes a house move, which means more to a child and his private world than adults often appreciate, may be the cause of a relapse of bed-wetting. Even the commonplace experience of going on holiday may upset him in this way. Similarly, when a child is around the age of three a mother often feels that at last she will be allowed a little more freedom, and can employ a baby-sitter. But if the child does not know the baby-sitter very well he may be worried and apprehensive. In other words, the mother knows the child-minder is quite competent and reliable, but the toddler himself is not so sure about it.

One of the most common causes for a persistently wet bed is parental displeasure after a temporary relapse from dryness. This may occur quite naturally, due to some brief but unavoidable tension, worry, changed routine of a type previously mentioned, or even an episode of illness. All too frequently the mother assumes it is just due to laziness, when in actual fact tonsillitis or some similar illness may have temporarily upset the delicate neurological balance.

Bed-wetting, or to look at the whole subject more positively, the absence of naturally dry beds in the morning – for surely even the most ill-informed person cannot seriously believe that any child likes this sort of discomfort – seems therefore to be directly related to anxiety in children, and to nothing else.

Reflex emptying of the bladder and the bowels is an automatic anxiety mechanism, and so there is every reason for an anxious child to wet the bed. But the whole miserable business does not stop there. On top of his anxiety he is sometimes made to feel degraded. He loses his self-confidence and feels ashamed, and so the condition rapidly becomes worse. In other words an element of depression now flavours his anxiety as well.

It is really quite amazing that this very straightforward state of affairs has been so insufficiently understood. For some years, doctors and parents have known that if a chronically bed-wetting child goes into hospital for investigation of his disability, he nearly always remains completely dry during this time. It is almost as if the child feels quiet for the first time in his life. He knows he is expected to wet the bed. Indeed he is in hospital because everyone expects him to do just that thing. And so he does not worry. He does not wet the bed either!

Other observed facts about this troublesome disability also point the finger towards anxiety as its fundamental and sole cause. It is known that in institutions and schools where a punitive attitude is taken whenever there is a wet bed in the dormitory, the trouble spreads rapidly. The infectious nature of anxiety has been stressed elsewhere in this book.

The prevention of bed-wetting therefore really is a straightforward thing, and must be centred around keeping a child in a position in which he can feel confident, especially around the age of three. Particular care should be taken to show that wet beds make not one iota of difference to anybody's attitude at home, and all temptations to make comparisons with other children's prowess must be resisted firmly.

Obviously punitive measures, like restricting fluid around bed-time, or disturbance at night, should be avoided like the plague. It is important too not to be unduly influenced by the child's own outlook towards his disability. Some children are quite unhappy and miserable about their plight, while others will assume a 'couldn't-care-less' attitude, and try to pretend that the problem does not exist. Finally, there are a number of children who, out of a hopeless sense of personal shame, become definitely obstructive and awkward in many other ways if they are made to feel guilty about bed-wetting. When this happens further regression can be expected, and day-wetting of clothes and soiling may occur.

Although as we have seen the medical profession has not been very efficient at solving the problems of the child who wets the bed, over the last few years treatment with drugs that are not generally used to reduce anxiety, have found favour. These are the anti-depressive drugs, like imipramine. A knowledge of the natural history of the disease will surely soon become more prevalent, and the use of these substances will not be called upon quite so much.

The importance of confidence in oneself cannot be over-emphasized in the fight we all must make from time to time against fear and anxiety. Many years ago a case mentioned in a book written about nervous children illustrated this very well, with reference to bed-wetting. A boy was very near being asked to leave a public school because of chronic bed-wetting. Out of desperation a portable rubber urinal was supplied to him, of a type normally used by incontinent men who suffer from prostate gland trouble. From the time this apparatus was given to the lad and he prepared himself to use it, his bed was permanently dry. And it was not because the portable urinal collected his night urine – in fact the bag was always empty in the morning – but because confidence had at last replaced fear. He felt sure that he would get over his disability.

Phobias (Especially School Phobia)
Phobias have already been discussed, and children suffer from phobic fears in rather the same way as do adults. Frequently the contagious quality of anxiety is particularly evident, and a mother's fear of the dark, of certain animals, insects, or for instance thunderstorms, may be easily imprinted upon a sensitive child's personality.

In recent years a special type of 'phobia' has been recognized in children, and really this is not a true phobia at all, but a simple dislike of, and an acute anxiety about school. I do not think there is any doubt that some cases of school phobia evolve because of simple, straightforward separation-anxiety. As we have seen, all children have their own rate of maturation. It is a highly individual thing, and yet still too many parents believe in going by chronological age alone when deciding upon exactly what a child is psychologically ready to face in the way of a test. In this way a toddler who is not ready for nursery school may be placed in such an environment simply because his sister took happily to it at the same age. But if he is not psychologically mature enough to make this change, the seeds of school phobia are sown.

The symptoms of this very common psychological ailment are often gastro-intestinal upsets and vomiting. Diarrhoea is probably the commonest symptom, and sometimes abdominal pains are complained of. Headache is another common symptom of school phobia, and it is important to realize that apart from occurring in infectious diseases as part and parcel of the high temperature reaction, headache is not a common symptom in young children. At times the child's complaints are bizarre in the extreme. One boy convinced his mother that he could not walk in the normal way at all, but could get around quite easily at home by moving sideways, and this was one of the rare times when I could confidently diagnose a disease over the telephone.

The treatment of toddlers with school phobia is straightforward and simple. They should be removed from the nursery school as soon as possible and given a period of six months at home again. Prevention is better than cure in all cases, and before a child is tried in a nursery school, he should be used to, and quite happy about spending two or three hours at a time away from his home and family.

School phobia after the age of five, when the child is expected to spend a while at least away from his mother, can be quite a problem. Most primary school teachers are very good at gaining the confidence of youngsters, many of whom are extremely anxious about the prospect of leaving home for the best part of the day. Parents should not be over-worried if a child seems to regress as far as general development is concerned as a result of school-induced anxiety, and bed-wetting, nail-biting, hair-twisting may occur and even the request to cuddle up or come into mother's bed may be expressed. Sometimes temporary school phobia crops up soon after an illness, and here absence from school should not be prolonged because of psychological symptoms.

On occasions, school phobia occurs much later on, when for instance, a child has been established at school for some time, or just after a change of school. In this instance the subject should be very carefully assessed. Sometimes bullying at school is the reason for the symptoms. The way in which a child is dressed or turned out for school may cause ridicule; overshined shoes and spotless shirts at a school where the average shirt is worn for a week and shoes are seldom if ever cleaned, can be an embarrassment.

The best way to handle the problem of bullies is probably not through the school, but by an individual confrontation with the child in question. Sometimes a few private lessons in self-defence, or even ju-jitsu, are a good idea before the confrontation occurs, but in any case a bully never does very well if invited to perform in front of an adult, and far away from his usual 'gang' of supporters.

On rare occasions a member of school staff, for a curious

reason of his own, picks on a child, and if this is suspected it must be put right. More frequently a child is put under too much pressure and is expected to do more than his capabilities will allow. This state of affairs often occurs in well-to-do families, in which an individual child's intellect is not comparable to that of his parents, or brothers and sisters. They cannot understand why a child of theirs is, in any way, backward at school, and finds the things he is expected to do quite beyond his ability.

For treatment of all forms of school phobia one must find the cause. In both human and animal experiments it has been proved without doubt that anxiety reduces the power to learn. A child with school phobia is already carrying a heavy load. If he is anxious about his school situation, whatever that may be, and anxious about being slow to learn, the worry about what his parents will be thinking of him is often the last straw. Plainly it is something to be avoided at all costs.

CHAPTER THIRTEEN

More than Anxiety

All through this book anxiety has been examined in its various guises, and we have seen how anxiety states are triggered off by many different things. Sometimes it has been due to looking at life almost as though through a distorting lens (reality fears, and states of mind brought about by denial of one's natural urge to be creative). At other times anxiety is set up by curious subconscious drives that we have designated, for want of a simpler classification to help us, as various false suppositions. Then again there has been anxiety that has had a purely physical basis.

In this way it has been possible to recognize the bare bones of anxiety in everyday life, and by recognizing them, know them for what they are – simple, everyday feelings experienced in some measure by us all, and in intolerable intensity in certain circumstances too.

Common as anxiety is, however, care must be taken not to confuse it with its rather more dangerous sister, depression. For not only is depression always a danger – it may well end in suicide if early diagnosis and adequate treatment are not forthcoming – but the management and treatment of the two states of mind are utterly different. Whereas self-knowledge and maturity can often help anxiety to evaporate, depression is always a matter for the doctor to deal with.

The diagnosis of depression is not always easy. Often it is already present in a malignant form before the victim is really aware of what is wrong with him. An early warning system for this dangerous disease is therefore clearly needed, leading to earlier diagnosis by relatives, friends and victims alike.

It is important to separate the everyday complaint of feeling depressed from an actual depressive illness. We all feel depressed at times. The day is grey and our spirits are at a low ebb; suddenly life seems uninviting, and work becomes a chore. Something has gone wrong, perhaps with our car, or the children have caught chicken pox. If the bank manager is anxious about our overdraft, we may feel justifiably depressed about this too. But in essence this is only a mood. Quite often it has been preceded by a mood of elation when it seemed that all the birds were singing, the sky was blue and life was very good.

A depressive illness is quite different. Often, as we have seen, anxiety precedes depression, and may be intimately associated with it. True depression slows a man or a woman down, and this slowing is both mental and physical. A depressed person's face is careworn. He looks much older than he is, the eyes appear wrinkled and dull. If left alone, there is a marked reduction of activity, and the patient sits about dully staring into space.

The slowness is often particularly noticeable in response to questioning, and the depressed person seems to find difficulty in rousing himself enough to reply to simple questions, such as 'How are you?' When he does reply the voice is toneless and often devoid of emotion. Sometimes tears well up in his eyes as he speaks.

Once conversation is established the depressed patient can usually describe his feelings accurately, if slowly. Sometimes he will say he feels hopeless, a man apart, or that he is sure he is dying, perhaps of cancer. Occasionally a depressed patient will be shy of mentioning his actual feelings of hopelessness, and therefore complains of a purely physical symptom, like backache or headache, that he feels will be more readily acceptable to those around him, rather than try to explain his terrible personal agony.

Many depressed women feel they are a 'disgrace'. Sometimes they dwell on quite minor sexual misdemeanours in the past, or may suddenly feel responsible for some member of the family's, or even a distant relative's personal troubles. In some people there is a distinct tendency to make mountains out of molehills, and the small personality defects that all of us have in one way or another are magnified and enlarged upon. The depressed person often feels he is a great burden to his family and friends, and then there is a real danger of suicide.

In an elderly person depression may appear first of all as a sudden lowering of standards of personal cleanliness, or a lack of any desire to dress properly or go to the lavatory when nature calls.

Although a depressed person will usually converse if pressed, there is a great reluctance to write a regular letter, for instance to a friend or relative, for someone in this state of mind seems to experience a complete mental block in this direction. An early and fairly constant sign of this illness is disturbance of sleep, in which early-morning waking is experienced. There is also great difficulty in waking up fully and getting going in the morning.

There are, of course, other more florid types of depression. The acute depressive is abject and dejected. He will never make a spontaneous remark, and may sit wringing his hands and weeping. In contrast to the mildly self-accusatory patient previously described, a patient in this condition will accuse himself if indeed he can be persuaded to make any comment about himself at all, of the most heinous crimes and wrong-doings. He also traces, sometimes, a patently impossible train of events in which almost everything that has gone wrong with his own, or his associates' lives, is claimed to be entirely his fault. As a dreadful wrongdoer he feels his only salvation is to be punished, but feels in his heart of hearts that even the worst punishment will be too good for him. In many cases he is convinced that his body is physically utterly rotten, corrupt and disgusting. He may even say that worms are eating his insides, or that his liver, brain, heart or bowels are hopelessly diseased. An extreme form of his type of depressive reaction is a state of virtual stupor, in which physical health is in great jeopardy, not because of a risk of suicide but due to profound inhibition of all life's vital processes.

It is unlikely that anyone would reach a severely depressed state of mind without someone, even the milkman or any other casual caller, noticing a profound change in the sick person's character. But minor degrees of depression are much more difficult to spot, and because of this are missed sometimes, even by the medical practitioner. Various schemes therefore have been put forward recently, to produce a relatively fool-proof screening procedure.

A workable instrument of this type has evolved, known as the Beck Depression Inventory. It is made up of a list of questions and answers relating to various aspects of depression. This is at present being used in only a relatively small number of trials. But already it seems as though it will enable people to spot depressive illness at an early stage, before serious or dangerous levels of depression are reached.

One of the reasons that doctors are keen to be able to diagnose their depressive patients as early as possible is that the cure of depression is comparatively easy these days, and that untreated depression has such a high mortality and morbidity rate.

This book is not the place for an examination of the details of any medical treatment, but effective therapy in depression involves many different types of treatment, including simple psychotherapy, use of mood-changing drugs and, on occasion, electroconvulsive therapy.

Finale

I have attempted to show where anxiety lurks and how it has the power to alter and spoil our lives, how it has its roots in the very nature of evolution, and that it is a primordial thing.

But because it is primordial this does not mean that man has no control over it. We know more about anxiety today than we have ever known. We can measure it and alter it. Some of the things that make us anxious seem curiously formless, and we can perhaps only recognize them by the shadows they cast on our personality. But by watching shadows and the way in which they alter under different circumstances we can often learn a lot about what is producing the darkness. So it is with anxiety. We may not be able to conquer it entirely, but we can learn ways of altering its pattern and curbing some of its destructive force.

All of us do odd things from time to time. The human being has not yet been made who behaves wholly rationally, and some of the irrationality of man is due to his anxiety. By realizing just this one thing, we make a step towards escaping from anxiety's worst terrors, and mastering the fear of fear itself.

The opposite of anxiety is confidence. Confidence will not come to us by pretending that anxiety does not exist, or by turning away from it. The control of anxiety starts with knowledge: that is, knowledge of what causes it, and of its natural place in life. There are useful social acts that insulate us from anxiety. The unselfish love of one person for another and the love and security that should be found in a family are examples that come immediately to mind. Giving one's time or even some of one's possessions to others often helps, and those who really involve themselves in philanthropy in a completely selfless way, know well its powerful medicine.

There is a danger, too, when we turn aside too abruptly from our own personal and cultural beliefs and rituals. It is a great pity that so much religious dogma has been involved with punishment and recruitment, when a belief in the essential divinity of man seems nearer to what might be true spiritual fulfilment.

Finally, we should never underestimate the power of laughter over anxiety. The jester, the harlequin and nowadays the professional humorist, always has a place in culture, for laughter destroys anxiety, and re-learning to laugh, perhaps even at ourselves, may answer many day-by-day anxieties. Jean Gebser has said that the ultimate conquest of anxiety is a smile, and that its radiance can mix shadow and light, fear and trust in such a way that a sort of harmony is created in which we can all participate.

If this little book provides some insight into how we can achieve this personal harmony with our fate, its writing will have been worthwhile.

Index

GEORGE ALLEN & UNWIN LTD

Head office:
40 Museum Street, London, W.C.1
Telephone: 01-405 8577

Sales, Distribution and Accounts Departments
Park Lane, Hemel Hempstead, Herts.
Telephone: 0442 3244

Athens: 7 Stadiou Street, Athens 125
Auckland: P.O. Box 36013, Northcote, Auckland 9, Central, N.4
Barbados: P.O. Box 222, Bridgetown
Beirut: Deeb Building, Jeanne d'Arc Street
Bombay: 103/5 Fort Street, Bombay 1
Calcutta: 285J Bepin Behari Ganguli Street, Calcutta 12
Cape Town: P.O. Box 2314 Joubert Park, Johannesburg, South Africa
Dacca: Alico Building, 18 Motljheel, Dacca 2
Delhi: 1/18B Asaf Ali Road, New Delhi 1
Hong Kong: 105 Wing on Mansion, 26 Hankow Road, Kowloon
Ibadan: P.O. Box 62
Karachi: Karachi Chambers, McLeod Road
Lahore: 22 Falettis' Hotel, Egerton Road
Madras: 2/18 Mount Road, Madras 2
Manila: P.O. Box 157, Quezon City D-502
Mexico: Liberia Britanica, S.A. Separo Rendon 125, Mexico 4DF
Nairobi: P.O. Box 30583
Rio de Janeiro: Caixa Postal 2537-Zc-00
Singapore: 36c Prinsep Street, Singapore 7
Sydney, N.S.W.: Bradbury House, 55 York Street
Tokyo: C.P.O. Box 1728, Tokyo 100-91
Toronto: 145 Adelaide Street West, Toronto 1

YOUR HEART AND HOW TO LIVE WITH IT

LAWRENCE E. LAMB

For many people *Your Heart and How to Live with It* will be the most important book they ever read. Dr Lamb, firmly convinced that the modern way of life has made heart disease largely the modern way of death, presents in this book a powerful case for his belief and tells what can be done to prevent heart disease. Not all physicians agree with Dr Lamb's viewpoint, but the evidence he provides is so strong that one will ignore it at one's peril.

After a brief review of the medical record, from rare case histories before 1910 when coronary heart disease was first recognized, to the latest comparative studies on its incidence among various populations, Dr Lamb covers the entire subject of the cardiovascular system and its ailments. He explains the anatomy of the heart and how it works; the role of the circulation and what happens when the blood vessels become diseased; and the physiological effects on heart function of bed rest, exercise, prolonged standing, and sexual activity, with helpful advice for everyone – including those who have had a heart attack. Among other factors that he soberly evaluates are the influence of smoking, alcohol, stress, heredity, and personality.

Of great practical value is an informative chapter on how to exercise properly to strengthen the heart without endangering it, and another on proper diets – either for losing weight or for maintaining it – to reduce the risk of heart attack, taking into account the latest research findings on cholesterol and saturated fats.

Dr Lamb also gives a summary of such problems as high blood pressure, angina pectoris, and valvular diseases, with their medical or surgical treatment, in addition to describing heart transplants and the current efforts to devise an artificial heart. Finally, there are simple, clear directions for administering artificial circulation to a victim of a heart attack who has lost consciousness, to keep him alive until professional help is available.

YOUR MIND CAN HEAL YOU

FREDERICK W. BAILES

There is a definite law of mental healing, and that this law can be applied to anyone, regardless of his mental strength or will-power, is conclusively demonstrated in this inspiring book. It is a practical introduction to the technique of mental and physical treatment. It is compatible with every religious belief; actually it is scientific rather than religious.

While a student at a large London hospital, Dr Bailes closely observed the mental factors which entered into the recovery of patients. He noticed that certain fundamental thought patterns invariably produced corresponding body reactions, and that he could produce these reactions by stimulating their causative mental patterns. Trained in the sciences, he reasoned that there must be similar certainty of action in the mental world. During the subsequent years he proved conclusively that both sickness and health find their origin in corresponding mental states, that there is a definite technique of mental and spiritual treatment which sets mental law in action and as a result brings physical health.

MIRAGE OF HEALTH

RENE DUBOS

'Complete freedom from disease and from struggle is almost incompatible with the process of living.' Hence, says the Rockefeller Institute's famous Dr Dubos, mankind's dream of perfect health for all in an antiseptic Eden is not only impossible, but impractical. And the aseptic world would be dangerous as well as woefully dull.

Dr Dubos unveils a medical panorama of incredible scope, embracing ancient and modern times; industrialized societies and savage tribes; animals; landscapes; and the commanding influence sickness has had on cultures, politics and warfare. He takes the reader on a journey where the unexpected and marvellous are encountered on virtually every page.

NERVES AND THEIR CURE

C. EDWARD BARKER

'What can I do for myself?' is the cry of every nervous patient. *Nerves and their Cure* provides a workable, down to earth answer. Free from technical jargon these pages give practical understanding and guidance to the victim of nervous trouble. He is enabled to get behind the scenes of his obsessions, phobias, hysterias, sleeplessness or depression and to recognize the 'pattern' that makes for his nervous tension, fatigue and breakdown.

But an intellectual grasp of his problem is not enough. This book helps the reader to acquire deep emotional 'insight' into the tricks of his unconscious mind, so that he can alter his nervous pattern of reaction and gain control and new health.

This insight comes by a variety of techniques he can practice himself. He learns how to observe his unconscious mind at work through the eyes of his dreams, his phantasies, his peculiarities. He learns the wise use of relaxation, the conditioned-reflex, and a healthy attitude to faith.

Here is an invaluable handbook of recovery for the nervous sufferer. It is also of special interest to students, doctors, nurses, psychiatric social workers, and not least to the harassed mothers of young children.

EMOTIONAL PROBLEMS OF LIVING

O. SPURGEON ENGLISH, M.D., and
GERALD H. J. PEARSON, M.D.

The authors in this book take the reader chapter by chapter through certain common experiences of life, so that by a process of *living with* the forces that make up a human personality we emerge with a closer understanding of human nature.

Emotional Problems of Living describes the different frictions generated within the individual or through his contacts with his environment. Its purpose is to give a point of view and a therapeutic approach which will reduce to a minimum those conflicts that tend toward the neurotic pattern. The book takes full cognizance of psychoanalytic thought, since the authors feel that Freudian psychoanalysis is the best approach to the understanding of personality. From birth to old age, the continuing development of the personality is discussed, and the reader is made familiar with the commoner deviations from the normal that occur at each particular period of life.